Praise for Future Driven

"David Geurin provides readers with a look into what our educational environments should truly look like. Throughout *Future Driven*, there are real stories that highlight the importance of overcoming obstacles, treating others with respect, and most importantly preparing students for the future. Get ready to be inspired and take immediate action as your work through this innovation manifesto geared towards promoting the success of all students."

—Brad Currie, 2017 NASSP National Assistant Principal of the Year

"Geurin manages to masterfully combine pedagogy, leadership, motivation, and riveting stories from his own experiences into one succinct book. Educators in any role will find great value in the pages of *Future Driven*. I couldn't put it down. It's essential reading for teachers and school leaders looking to transition their thinking from "Bear" to "Bull" and "make learning irresistible."

—Weston Kieschnick, Author of *Bold School*
Senior Fellow, International Center for Leadership in Education

"This book is a must-read for every educator! David's passion for teaching and learning collide with a vision for future-ready schools in an authentic way that makes you feel like David's in the room and talking with you over a cup of coffee. This is a book that provides many practical examples, inspires a can-do attitude, and ignites a sense of urgency to think differently about what it means to prepare students for success in their futures."

—Jennifer Hogan, Assistant Principal of Curriculum and Technology
Hoover High School, Alabama

"David Geurin doesn't hold back! Through his experiences and connections with other leaders, Geurin weaves stories and advice for educators to create a true, future-driven focus for student success!"

—Neil Gupta, Director of Secondary Education, Worthington City Schools

"If you know David, you know he is speaks boldly and plainly for advancing what we do in changing learning and teaching for the betterment of all. This project is view into the practical and impactful change practices his school embraces and a glimpse into the future of learning. This is a powerful tool!"

—Derek McCoy, Principal West Rowan Middle School NASSP National
Digital Principal Award Winner

"Thought provoking and informative, *Future Driven* asks the important questions to ensure that our students will be successful in an ever-changing world. Geurin outlines ways educators can fine tune their thinking to lead innovation and gives practical examples of how to be effective change agents."

—Winston Y. Sakurai, Ed.D
2016 NASSP National Digital Principal Award Winner
2016 HASSA Hawaii State Secondary Principal of the Year

"In *Future Driven,* David Geurin provides practical strategies that can immediately be applied no matter your title in education. As a school leader, my thinking was pushed to new heights with each turn of the page. *Future Driven* is a must-read for educators looking to transform practices to meet the needs of students now and for years to come. This will be a book that I return to for inspiration and ideas over and over again."

—Beth Houf, co-author of *Lead Like a PIRATE*
National Distinguished Principal of Fulton Middle School

Download the FREE Discussion Guide and Bonus Resources

Ready to take action?
Just to say thanks for buying my book,
I'd like to give you...
A Discussion Guide,
A Suggested Reading List,
My Curated Video Resources,
And More.

GO TO HTTP://BIT.LY/FUTUREDRIVEN
TO DOWNLOAD YOUR RESOURCE KIT.

Future Driven

WILL YOUR STUDENTS THRIVE IN AN
UNPREDICTABLE WORLD?

David Geurin

#FutureDriven

David G. Geurin
4404 S. 146th Rd.
Bolivar, MO 65613
www.davidgeurin.com

Book Layout ©2017 BookDesignTemplates.com

Ordering Information:
Quantity sales. Special discounts are available on quantity purchases by corporations, associations, and others. For details, contact the author at the address above.

Future Driven, David Geurin
ISBN 9780692916278

Contents

CHAPTER 1

Shaping the Future

I was in a classroom last summer that looked just like the ones I attended when I was in school. And I wasn't visiting a museum. But it was practically the same as classrooms from decades ago, with just a couple of differences. An LCD projector was mounted to the ceiling, connected to a computer on the teacher's desk. Oh and one other thing. It didn't have a chalkboard; it had a white marker board.

But other than that, it looked like any classroom from years ago. All the desks were in neat rows. The teacher's desk was at the front of the room. There were posters on the walls with historical information but nothing to really indicate any issues facing our modern world. All the textbooks were stacked neatly on the shelves for summer break.

And while this classroom was probably more extreme than most in its imitation of a time capsule, there are too many classrooms and schools that aren't coming close to keeping up with the rate of change in the world around us. In fact, hardly any schools are keeping up with the rate of change. It's nearly impossible.

Things are changing so fast in our complex and uncertain world it makes it difficult to know exactly what students need for their future. The challenges we are facing are significant. So even schools that are trying to keep up are actually still falling behind.

The old rules don't apply.

Time Capsule or Time Machine

Schools should be less like time capsules and more like a time machine. Now before you think I'm suggesting we spend our school budgets on DeLoreans and try to replicate what Doc Brown and Marty McFly accomplished in Back to the Future, please hear me out. What I mean is that educators should always have an eye on the future. My time machine metaphor isn't about visiting the past. Since we are charged with helping students prepare for the world they will live in, we must think about what that world will be like, what it will demand, what it will take to thrive in Tomorrowland. Educators should be futurists.

Futurists are scientists or social scientists who look ahead at what might be possible. They don't necessarily try to predict the future. No one can do that. But they explore all of the possibilities of how current realities might lead to future developments in any and all areas of life.

Every person can have a time machine in a sense. By thinking like a futurist, we can ponder with imagination and wonder what the future might be like, and almost travel there ourselves. And as educators, we can seek to create schools that not only reflect our modern world, but prepare students for the uncertainties of tomorrow. To be a futurist, you must also reflect on the past. It is the foundation upon which progress is built. But the time machine approach does not live in the past, and it is not driven by the past. This time machine is future-driven.

By contrast, the time capsule approach only protects the status quo. It assumes that the way we were taught is good enough for today's students too. Certainly, there were elements of my 80's education that were timeless. There were teachers who inspired me, who helped me develop a love of learning, and who taught me to solve problems. I am grateful for the outstanding teachers I had as a student.

But there were also parts of my education that fell short. Why can't we be honest about this? Especially when we consider how different the world is today. For the most part, my education was a passive experience. I spent many hours bored with school and thinking about other things that were more interesting to me.

I have always been a dreamer, but there were few opportunities in my school experience to explore my passions or my dreams. For the most part, my teachers "taught" me and I sat and "learned." My voice was not needed, and my unique gifts were not valued. As a result, I truly learned just a fraction of what was taught, and I was a good student. Much of what I learned was forgotten soon after it was regurgitated on exams.

Do not confine your children to your own learning for they were born in another time. —Chinese Proverb

Why Adaptable Learners Will Own the Future

When I was a little kid, my grandpa bought me a pony. I know that sounds like the type of gift a spoiled rich kid might get. But we were definitely not rich. Grandpa owned a small farm in rural West Kentucky where he and my grandma worked tirelessly to make a living. And just a few miles from the family farm was a state park where an auction was being held to sell off some surplus items, and the pony happened to be one of the items they were selling.

We named the pony Snowball for obvious reasons. He was white from head to tail with a round belly like a snowball. But Snowball had some bad habits. The reason the state park owned her, to begin with, was that she was part of the pony rides. Any time she had a saddle and a rider, she was conditioned to walk in circles. She knew how to do her job very well. Simply walk in a circle all day long. I guess you could say she was literally a "one trick pony." No doubt my grandpa got a bargain on this majestic steed!

Snowball didn't respond well-being led in a straight line, and she certainly wasn't used to having a rider take the reins. One time, when I was in the saddle, a loud truck drove by and she was startled. As I remember it, she reared up and bucked me right off. In my imagination, I was certain I could hang on like the Lone Ranger. In reality, even this little pony was more than I could handle.

As I was reflecting on Snowball's limitations, I thought about how the world is changing for our students. In the past, it was possible to learn a skill or trade and remain in the same career for a lifetime. Those opportunities have mostly disappeared. Even more of these jobs will be gone in the coming years. It's not possible to be a "one-trick pony" anymore.

In today's world, information is abundant and automation is accelerating. To possess a variety of skills that cross a multitude of disciplines is critical for success. Things are changing so quickly that it is impossible to keep up. And that is why adaptable learners will own the future.

We cannot predict with certainty all of the knowledge and skills our students will need. Preparing students for a test, or college, or even a trade isn't enough to be future ready.

Even though the job market has improved slightly for college grads in the last couple of years, 1 in 5 college graduates will find themselves unemployed or underemployed—working in low-wage fields that don't require a degree.

That is why we must develop skills that are transferable to unknown situations. As futurist Alvin Toffler noted, the ultimate 21st Century skill is the ability to "learn, unlearn, and relearn." It is a tremendous advantage to be creative, innovative, and adaptable.

College and Career Ready vs. Life Ready

Much has been made of the need for students to be college and career ready. Who could argue with that? Of course, we want students to graduate with the skills they need to be successful in college and career. One problem with this is that college and career readiness, as defined by accountability standards, is largely determined by standardized test scores. Anyone working with high school students could tell you stories of students who have high standardized test scores who are not ready for college or career. And conversely, there are also many students with lower standardized test scores who thrive in college or a career.

A perfect example of this was a former student who performed poorly on the ACT, far below what is considered a college and career ready score. But this student never thought to let a low ACT score stand in his way. He was an excellent citizen of the school community, participated in activities and athletics, and was well liked by classmates. Upon graduation, he was almost immediately employed and thriving in his work. And he soon started his own business on the side, too. Clearly, he was life-ready even though the test score said he wasn't.

As I reviewed our school's ACT results (in recent years, all Missouri juniors were required to take the test), there were many students whose scores were below the 'readiness' threshold who I am confident will do quite well in pursuing further education or in pursuing other meaningful opportunities upon graduation. And there also some with higher scores I worry about.

Of course, we always want our students to score as well as possible on the ACT or other exams, but we also respect that they may not place a high personal value on the tests. Achieving a certain ACT score may not be relevant to their goals. And they may have other skills that allow them to have the life they want without the need to score well on a timed college entrance exam.

College and career readiness cannot be adequately measured by a standardized test. But why limit readiness to college and career in the first place?

A bigger concern for me is to ensure students are life-ready or future-ready. Our students are more than future employees. And life is more than earning a paycheck. College and career readiness is concerned only with how students succeed in their ability to get a job. While the ability to support oneself and one's family is very important, it is also important to be a contributing member of a community, to participate in our democracy, to make a difference in the world, and to be a continuous learner.

Beyond test scores, educators should always be most concerned about helping students become successful adults. Education is an investment in a life, not a number. It seems like the emphasis in education recently has been on numbers, not the individual the number represents. *It's impossible to reduce a person's potential or performance to a number.*

Are standardized tests a good predictor of life success? I don't think they are. Sure, I think academic skills are a piece of a complex tapestry of what is takes to be successful. School should help students grow into effective all-around people. It's not just preparing students for college or career. School shouldn't just help students make a living, it should also help them make a life.

Adaptable 100 Years Ago

My grandparents married nearly 100 years ago. My grandad had a 6th-grade education. My grandmother went further in school, but still never graduated from high school.

Just prior to the onset of the Great Depression, they signed a banknote and purchased a piece of land for $1000. Perfect timing to launch an enterprise and take on debt, right? Like so many others in rural America, farming was how they intended to make a living. And they did. And it was by the sweat of their brow.

They were successful because they sacrificed. They worked tirelessly and helped others in their community. Things got done because of sheer will and never ending hard work. They fostered relationships with neighbors and family who were also trying to survive. They all survived by helping each other carve a living off the land.

I only knew my granddad when I was a young boy. But growing up I heard stories about him from others. He valued hard work almost to a fault. I don't know how many times someone who knew him would say to me, "You're Rudolph Geurin's grandson? Oh, he was one of the hardest workers I've ever known." Of course, that made me very proud.

The need to adapt is not new. It has always been important to think critically and creatively—to solve problems and handle challenges. My grandparents were determined people. They had grit. But they were also willing to take risks and try something new. They grew corn, wheat, soybeans, milo, and more. And they raised cattle, hogs, and even chinchillas for a short time. They were enterprising. They tried different things. And they faced challenges like drought, crop and livestock disease, and poor markets. Still, they were able to adapt.

But adaptability skills are even more relevant today. The skills are more complex because the world is more complex. Change is accelerating.

Where work in the past was manual and routine, now it involves complex thinking and communication. But let's be clear—adaptability is not entirely new.

We have motives both timeless and contemporary to nurture flexibility in our students.

Pay Attention

In 2005, I was a new administrator right out of my gig of teaching high school English. We moved to a new town, I started doctoral studies, and I was now the principal of a small, rural school with 280 students in grades 7-12.
At one point, I was the principal, a girls' basketball coach, and an after school program director—all at the same time. I wanted to drive a bus route too, but they wouldn't let me.

I remember feeling a tremendous weight of responsibility. Tremendous with a capital T. And I was trying to learn as much as I could.

During those years, I attended a technology conference where I saw a video, *Did You Know?* (https://youtu.be/ljbI-363A2Q) by Karl Fisch (@karlfisch) and later modified by Scott McCleod (@mcleod). It grabbed my attention. The video outlined the rapid changes happening in the world, how the internet was changing everything, how the world was more connected than ever before, how the old rules didn't apply.

The message I took from that video is one I carry forward in this book. The world is rapidly changing. It's essential we prepare students for the world they will live in and not the one we grew up in. Efforts to change learning for the better continue. But I wonder how much progress we've really made. How will you help your students learn to thrive in this unpredictable world?

Future Ready

If we want our students to be future-ready[1], then schools and educators need to be future-driven. It's not just preparing students to compete in a new economy, the so-called 4th Industrial Revolution. Future driven leaders want to ensure that students are prepared to thrive in all aspects of life. It's important for students to reach their potential and be lifelong learners. Students must *be ready* in a whole variety of ways.

Ready to serve.

Ready to empathize.

Ready to create hope.

Ready to be an engaged citizen.

Ready to think.

Ready to show responsibility.

Ready to seek justice.

Ready to be an upstander and not a bystander.

Ready to dream.

Ready to accept differences.

Ready to press forward when it gets tough.

Ready to adapt to change

It's not our future we are preparing our students for, but theirs. We can ill afford to prepare them for a world that won't exist. —Eric Sheninger

Driven

It's great to want *readiness* for our students. We want to prepare for what's next. We want them to be ready. But as educators, we have the opportunity to go beyond just preparing students for what's to come. We have the opportunity to work with students to help shape the future now. We aren't just preparing for something unknown and unpredictable that will happen.

We're ready! Some changes are on the way. It's gonna be really different. It'll be challenging. But we'll be ready for it. There are some big problems that will need solving. We'll just hang out here in school and get ready for someday. We'll just learn technology and prepare and get ready.

No. Absolutely not.

We are shaping what that future will look like right now. Schools have a chance to do stuff that matters for making the future brighter right now. So future-ready is a good thing, but we must be future driven—right now.

Time-capsule teachers clinch their fists and hang on to the past. Time-machine teachers are going places. They are taking their students places too. Encourage your students to become fascinated with the future. Make them restless for change. Be driven. Now. Be on a mission. Now. Solve real solve problems. Now.

Seek new possibilities.

Now.

Design Challenge

The traditional classroom I mentioned earlier was without students or teacher. It was summer break. I didn't have the opportunity to experience the true learning culture of this classroom.

But based on the classroom design, I made some assumptions about the other design choices the teacher might be making. Teachers are designers. This book will challenge you to design learning around experiences that are relevant for the world your students face, an increasingly unpredictable world.

It will further challenge educators to design schools and systems that encourage creativity and adaptability in learning. It's not enough for our students to simply master standards. Our world is too uncertain and the needs of today's learners are too complex for that type of thinking.

If our goal is to develop adaptable learners, we must start by creating adaptable schools. If we want students to be equipped to handle change, we need schools to embrace a culture of change. It's not acceptable to do things as they've always been done, and then expect results are going to be different.

If our goal is to develop adaptable learners, we must start by creating adaptable schools.
#FutureDriven

This book is filled with ideas to push your thinking because we need educators to think differently. To think like futurists. To consider how things could be different. To imagineer learning experiences that will help students be ready for anything.

Perspective

We see things. But we don't always see things as they are. Our vision is clouded by our own filters. We are limited to our own perspective. Often we're too close or too far away to make good sense of what we see. And there aren't workshops for educators on seeing clearly.

We want a strategy that can be used tomorrow. We want the handout, the cheat sheet, the quick fix. The hack. We want solutions that can be tossed in the microwave and heated up when we need them. Even if they taste like crap.

But the best solutions aren't microwave-friendly. They come through deliberate practice. They come through deeper thinking. They come by shifting perspective. So kick the quick fix to the curb. Do the hard work of challenging the status quo. Ponder the deeper questions and look at the world in new and interesting ways.

Question everything.

The Missing Map

If you're reading this book hoping for a formula or a road map with step-by-step instructions, you picked the wrong book. No cheats, hacks, or microwaved thinking. The goal here is to shift perspective. To think deeply. To break rules and barriers and ultimately move forward.

You will find lots of ideas for your classroom or school. As you encounter the ideas I share, use them to create your own personal map. A map that works for your classroom or school. A map you create to guide your actions.

What you do is important. Who you become is even more important. You need to consider how you will adapt to the changes inevitable in our world. When you initiate change in your sphere of influence, you help to invent the future. You aren't just reacting to change; you are anticipating it.

Clearly, you won't invent the future large scale, but you can invent a thin slice. You can use your platform to ensure students are future driven and able to adapt. You can help them make their own map.

If someone claimed a step-by-step guide to becoming an adaptable learner, it would be a false claim. The world is far too complex and the ability to lead and learn too important to trust to a set of instructions.

Better schools are built on better thinking. Future-driven educators must question the way things are and always consider if there is a better way? What do our students really need? What do we need to start doing? What do we need to stop doing? What do we need to do differently? In what ways can I change to help students be ready for an unknown future?

We need to be problem-finders and problem-solvers. But better thinking is not enough. We must take our ideas and translate them into actions. How can I make better decisions? What will I do next to make things better for students?

How will I create a future-driven classroom?

What good is an idea if it remains an idea. Try. Experiment. Iterate. Try again. Change the world. —Simon Sinek

CHAPTER 2

The Unexpected

❝**I** feel like I'm going to die."
She lay in our bed writhing in pain, fever raging. Her eyes told the story. Those big, beautiful brown eyes, always so full of life. Now they looked tired, desperate, and broken. I didn't know what to do. The doctors didn't know what to do.

I prayed. God, please help my wife. Heal her body.

Lori had suffered like this for months. She was so weak she could barely get out of bed. It took a great effort for her to rise. She would slowly push herself to her feet. When she walked, it was like she was 80 years old. She shuffled along, taking each step with concerted effort.

Her breathing was labored. She would try to take deep breaths, but it was never enough. "I feel like I can't get any air," she said.

She did her best to push through the pain. She rarely complained and still kept many of her responsibilities at home and work, in spite of the dreadful illness. Lori worked for the Exceptional Pupil Cooperative, a consortium of 15 school districts providing special education services to students in rural Southwest Missouri. She traveled to schools as an itinerant speech and language teacher, serving preschool children with special needs.

We talked about her quitting her job or taking more leave. She had missed some days for the illness, but for the most part, she would somehow find the strength to go on. Our four kids knew mom was sick of course, but they didn't know the full extent of it. She was determined to push forward. She didn't let it keep her from being a great mom and wife. She has an unstoppable spirit.

Eighteen long months after the onset of her illness, we finally had some answers. Lori first became sick after two different tick bites in the spring of 2012. She spent much of the following months researching possibilities, and her symptoms were certainly consistent with a tick-borne illness. Our suspicions were finally confirmed. After visits to five different doctors and dozens of tests, she was diagnosed with chronic Lyme disease.

It was validating for Lori to have a clear diagnosis. We had wondered if it was Lyme disease for so long. But the doctors weren't convinced. "You can't get Lyme disease in Missouri," they said. "Maybe you're just stressed?" Or, "You need to take walks."

It was incredibly frustrating. We felt like no one would help her.

But now the blood tests confirmed it was Lyme. Although the diagnosis was a step in the right direction, the battle wasn't over. Chronic Lyme disease is a mysterious illness, and the treatment options are limited. She continued to suffer from the disease in spite of antibiotic treatments, complicated herbal protocols, and strict organic diets.

Although Lori's health eventually improved, she still has flare-ups often. She had to quit her job. The physical demands of driving to various schools and working with preschoolers were too much. She has to be very careful about her energy level. When she exerts herself too much, it costs her for days. Lyme disease forced us to find a new normal for life in our family. We had to adapt.

Every person has to deal with the unexpected in life. We make plans. We have dreams. We want everything to work out just the way we want. And then life happens. You get a cancer diagnosis. You lose your job. Your child has autism. A tragedy takes the life of a loved one. Divorce rips your family apart.

Life is filled with challenges and all of our hopes and dreams are subject to the uncertainties of the future. We can't always predict what is going to happen. Even though we try our hardest to create security and do all the right things to take care of our loved ones, life always throws curves. We have to play the hand we're dealt. Life is about adjusting, being flexible, and meeting the challenges as they come.

Progress

The ability to rise to the challenge has always been essential to success. But how can we claim things are so hard today, right? We have modern conveniences like automobiles, electricity, and air conditioning. My grandparents went without indoor plumbing. Medical care was limited and when available, it was provided by a country doctor who probably had very little formal training.

It's amazing to think about the wonders of our modern world. I remember a time before the internet. I remember when we thought that having a microwave oven in our home was pretty much the greatest invention ever. A cordless phone was an amazing innovation. But those once new technologies are no comparison to the level of advancement we see now. We live in a time of unparalleled convenience, customization, and instant gratification.

But we're just getting started. More innovations are on the way. The news of what's just over the horizon is even more amazing. Cars are going to drive themselves. In fact, some already are. The Honda and Chevrolet both have technology that allows semi-autonomous driving, or adaptive cruise. But soon, cars will be entirely self-driving. Automation will create incredible efficiencies that will redefine jobs as we know them. Artificial intelligence and virtual reality will be integrated into daily life like never before.

But progress will also bring increased complexity. What jobs will be available? Will there be a greater disparity between the rich and the poor? How will rapid change impact political, social, and economic realities? Will robots take over the world? That's a scary thought unless they are taking over just the parts we want, like cutting the grass and folding our laundry.

Because of the uncertainties we face, it is very difficult to plan for tomorrow. According to a World Economic Forum Report, 7.1 million jobs could be lost in the next five years because of automation. But those losses could be at least partially offset by 2.1 million new jobs related to technology.[1]

In addition, we face significant problems related to overpopulation, pollution, melting ice caps, antibiotic resistant bacteria, and fierce clashes of religion, race, and culture. Just to name a few.

We must be forward-thinking. Schools need to prepare students for the major shifts that are happening. We can't be looking in the rear view mirror for solutions. We can't try to replicate the practices of the past. We must be future-driven.

Daniel Pink wrote about how a different type of thinking is needed in the future. In his book *A Whole New Mind*[2] he describes the impact of these significant changes:

> Mere survival today depends on being able to do something that overseas knowledge workers can't do cheaper, that powerful computers can't do faster. And what we do must satisfy nonmaterial, transcendent desires of this abundant age.

> The skills in greatest demand will be those that can't be replicated by a machine or can't be outsourced for a lower wage. It is essential to be an adaptable learner in a world of uncertainty and complexity.

> The future belongs to a very different kind of person with a very different kind of mind—creators and empathizers, pattern recognizers, and meaning makers.

Crystal Ball

Earlier I suggested educators must think like futurists. It's vital for educators to contemplate how the world might be different. We must do our very best to help students prepare for what's possible in their future.

However, it's impossible to predict the future with certainty. We don't have a crystal ball. We must help our students be ready for anything. To an extent, we must expect the unexpected.

But too often people (educators included) don't want to consider the realities of our changing world at all. It's frightening. The evidence of change might not coincide with a vision of the future they would like to see. It makes them uncomfortable. They worry about their own job. They worry about how technology might do harm. Sure, you like some of the conveniences of technology, but you don't want our lifestyle to change too much. You want the time capsule. You want predictability.

Try to put aside these fears and think about the future in positive ways. It's a proactive approach. We can take actions to position ourselves to handle the future if we are willing to look ahead. While challenges abound, there are also amazing opportunities. Be willing to adjust to the changes that are happening, and prepare to take advantage of new opportunities.

World Changers

Treat your students like they are world changers <u>now</u>.

No doubt they will inherit problems that are complex and far-reaching. But you never know when one of your students might find the cure for cancer, develop better energy solutions, or start a movement that leads to peace.

Treat **_all_** of them like they are world changers. I know there are students who are difficult, disrespectful, and disengaged. But don't let that place limits on what they might accomplish someday. Believe in their possibilities and build on their strengths.

Treat your students like they are world changers now. #FutureDriven

The future will have unexpected twists and turns. You never know how your influence might impact the life of one of your students. I showed a YouTube video to my staff with a powerful message.[3]

A young boy in an underdeveloped country is caught stealing food from a market. He is being treated harshly by the woman who caught him, but a kind shopkeeper intervenes on his behalf. He overlooks the boy's stealing and actually gives him a small bag of food to take to his sick mother. Over the years, the kind shopkeeper helps the boy from time to time.

Many years later, the kind shopkeeper is gravely ill and has accumulated tremendous hospital bills, and his daughter is unsure how to pay for her father's medical care. She is seen grieving her father's health and weeping over the ever growing debts.

But in a climactic moment, she opens the latest bill from the hospital to see the balance due is zero. The young boy her father helped over the years went on to be very successful, and he gives back to the old man who had helped him, even when he didn't deserve it.

Focus on what students are becoming, not just on who they are right now. You can see things in them they don't see in themselves. You can help bring out the best in them.

They might just change the world.

**Focus on what students are becoming,
not just on who they are right now.
#FutureDriven**

Focus on what students are becoming, not just on who they are right now. #FutureDriven

The American Dream

We'll think of the faith of our parents that was instilled in us here in America, the idea that if you work hard and play by the rules, you'll be rewarded with a good life for yourself and a better chance for your children. Filled with that faith, generations of Americans have worked long hours on their jobs and passed along powerful dreams to their sons and daughters. Many of us can remember our own parents working long hours on their jobs and then coming home and helping us with our homework. The American dream has always been a better life for people who are willing to work for it. —President Bill Clinton, 1993

You go to school. You make good grades. You get a good job.

You play by the rules.

Our school system is designed like this. Show up. Listen. Follow instructions. Do what you're told. Take notes.

Study for your tests. Try hard. Do your homework.

In school, you stand out by being the best at fitting in. But life isn't like that, not anymore. Too many college grads are delivering pizzas or working in call centers.

I was taught the value of hard work. And hard work counts. A person who works hard deserves respect and a good living. But hard work doesn't guarantee success.

Bringing value to others leads to increased chances for success. The American Dream is still alive in my thinking. But hard work is just the starting point. How else can you add value? What problem will you solve? What will be your gift to the world?

Think Like a Futurist

An essential message of this book is that educators must think forward. We need to consider how our students need to be ready for whatever life throws at them, including the unexpected things that can derail a future. As technology continues to drive change, new challenges will emerge, but new opportunities will abound.

Here are five steps educators can use to think like a futurist:

1. Always be willing to challenge how you are doing things right now.

It may seem like this is focused on what's happening in your present situation, but when we reject the status quo and really examine our current practices critically, we are being future-driven. We must be open to change and the idea that there is probably a better way to do everything.

2. Read the news with an eye on the future.

The news is filled with hints about what is coming in the future. Of course, there will be surprises. But when we stay abreast of trends and innovations, it really helps us be a step ahead of what's coming. Some things are obvious. Technology is going to play a major role in the direction of change. But as you read more about future related topics, you will be able to make inferences about what the future may hold.

3. Constantly reflect on ways to help your students be adaptable.

No matter where we hit or miss about the future, one thing is certain: the ability to adapt is always valuable. Think about how this impacts teaching and learning. Students need to practice solving complex problems and challenging themselves to do things that are uncomfortable at first.

4. Share ideas with your students and other educators about what the future may demand.

We can turn our schools into adaptable cultures, always keeping an eye on the future and how it is changing and then share it with others. If people in your school start to have conversations about information relevant to the future, it creates a flow. That information is helpful to decision-making and mindsets.

5. Embrace the future even when it's hard.

Some aspects of what the future might hold aren't promising. Sometimes, they are downright frightening. But we need to embrace the future, not because we like everything about it, but because we need to be prepared for it. We need to have the skills to thrive in a complex world. And we need to help our students develop these skills too.

Failed Time Machine

I've asked you to think like a futurist. But I need to share just how terrible I am at looking around corners. It's not that I don't look to the future, it's just that I don't always see it clearly. As I mentioned before, none of us has a crystal ball.

When I first heard the idea of online college courses years ago, I didn't think it would work, especially to earn a degree. Well, online learning exceeds $100 billion now. I've taught online courses myself for almost a decade.

And then there's Twitter. I scoffed at this idea. Why would they limit you to 140 characters? It'll never work. But now I can't imagine not having the benefit of the connections and learning I get from Twitter.

Those are just a couple of examples. Too often I've been skeptical and failed to have the vision to see what's possible.

When things are changing so quickly, it's tough to predict what's next. The key is to be looking forward and paying attention. Then, chart your course based on your best guess, and the best guesses of others. Consider all of the possibilities of what change might bring and position yourself as well as you can.

One thing is for sure, you can't be static and do nothing and let change happen to you. You have to be part of driving change. Do something even if it's wrong.

Take a risk.

Adaptable learners aren't passive. They are on the move. Even when they get it wrong, they are able to adjust quickly. Passive learners are dust in the wind. Think inertia—a body in motion tends to stay in motion. A body at rest tends to stay at rest.

Disruption

Uber, the world's largest taxi company, owns no vehicles. Facebook, the world's most popular media owner, creates no content. Alibaba, the most valuable retailer, has no inventory. And Airbnb, the world's largest accommodation provider, owns no real estate. Something interesting is happening. —Tom Goodwin

You can bet these companies have made their conventional rivals very uncomfortable. Taxi companies are fighting Uber. Newspapers are struggling to retain advertisers. They didn't see this coming. It was obvious to everyone, but most of them completely ignored the change. They didn't want to see it coming.

Educators are uncomfortable too. We tend to hold on to prior ways because they are more comfortable or because they correspond to a version of the future we want. You may not like the changes you see with technology. You may not like the shifts in economics, politics, culture, etc. Sometimes we don't want to face reality because we just don't like it. You are attached to an outcome. And you make decisions accordingly, even in the face of evidence to the contrary.

But that doesn't make your day go better, or make you more effective, or help you adapt to the changes we face. You need to take a different perspective and challenge your own assumptions. The adaptable learner doesn't just build a case to support what she hopes to be true. She adjusts the sails to deal with the changing winds.

Never Give Up

Resilience and perseverance are some of the most important skills we learn in life. There will always be doubters. There will be obstacles and challenges. There will be people who will try to put limits on what you can do. They will try to steal your dreams. Some of our greatest heroes had to overcome incredible obstacles to achieve greatly. That's what makes them heroes. They didn't always get it right the first time. They weren't perfect. Life wasn't always easy. And yet they didn't give up.

I think it's important to share our stories with our students and let them know the challenges we faced. We should also invite them to share their stories and celebrate the moments of determination and resilience. We want to teach students to be overcomers. We want them to be emotionally strong. It's the only way to succeed in a complex, rapidly changing world.

In my own life, I faced numerous setbacks and disappointments. There were times when I felt overlooked or misunderstood. And there are times I let those difficulties slow me down. But I never quit. I always bounced back and kept moving forward. These challenges didn't define my future.

I was held back in 2nd grade because I wasn't succeeding in the classroom. I think I was a pain in my teacher's neck...or pick another part of the anatomy.

I was bullied relentlessly throughout junior high and was the 'fat' kid. I often dreaded going to school and can remember feeling hopeless after some of the things that were said or done to me.

Our family moved three times while I was in high school so I never stayed anywhere too long. It was difficult to make lasting friendships, and I often felt like an outsider.

Although I was an average high school basketball player, I made a failed attempt to play college basketball. Actually, I was briefly on the team, but I never fulfilled my dream of actually playing at the college level.

As a young teacher, I was placed on an 'improvement plan,' and I totally deserved it. And ultimately, I learned from this humbling experience.

I applied unsuccessfully for a number of principal or assistant principal jobs before a school finally took a chance on me.

After getting my first principal job, a former supervisor commented to a colleague, "I didn't know if he'd make it as a principal. I thought it could go either way."

No matter what you or your students are going through, never give up. Our lives are not shaped by our circumstances nearly as much as they are shaped by how we respond to our circumstances. Even the difficulties can be used to make us better. As Rick Warren says often, the difficulties can "make us bitter, or they make us better."

Never. Give. Up.

Be a Fighter

We can't know everything our students are going to need to be ready for their futures. And it's not enough to just prepare them for the next grade level or for college. We must create adaptable learners. We must BE adaptable learners.

At times, Lori has been so sick she just wanted to give up. She wanted to quit trying because it felt like she was never going to feel better. It felt like there wasn't any hope. She wasn't prepared for Lyme disease. You don't expect to have a struggle like that. But I'm proud of her because she is a fighter, and she has pressed on in spite of the challenges. She found ways to adapt and continue to believe and find hope.

As our world becomes increasingly complex and uncertain, we know schools need to adapt to the changes. It won't always be easy. The problems we face are mounting. Educators carry a heavy load. And doing what's best for students isn't always what's most comfortable for adults.

But all educators need to keep fighting for the most relevant, authentic learning experiences possible for our students. They are counting on us.

We must keep fighting. We must get comfortable being uncomfortable. We must help our students prepare for the unexpected.

**Doing what's best for students isn't always
what's most comfortable for adults.
#FutureDriven**

CHAPTER 3

What If Schools Were More Like Google or Starbucks?

What can education learn from companies that are leaders of innovation and knowledge creation in their industries? Can the culture of these organizations translate to education to help create even better opportunities for students? In our rapidly changing world, the need for new paradigms and creative thinking is more important than ever.

Schools that will thrive in the future won't do what's always been done. They won't simply replicate success; instead, they will invent new ideas of how schools can help students be future-ready.

In business, adaptability is the new competitive advantage.[1] Failure to adapt has doomed a number of companies. Schools must be adaptable in order to meet the needs of students who need skills to manage change in this complex world. One study revealed that 91% of HR managers consider the ability of a candidate to deal with change a major recruitment goal.[2]

Bulls and Bears

Bull

Twenty years ago, there was no Google. Today its search engine is the most visited website in the world, and it's one of the most valuable brands in the world, worth hundreds of billions. But Google is far more than a search engine these days. The company continues to innovate and adapt.

Bear

Once the most popular website in the world, Yahoo has been in persistent decline for more than a decade. At the start, Yahoo wanted to charge for email and other services while Google was providing services for free. But its biggest misstep was failing to adapt to mobile. AOL, Netscape, MySpace, and Napster are other once great tech companies that eventually flamed out.

Bull

Netflix has shown its ability to adapt. Initially, it was exclusively a DVD-subscription service. But Netflix recognized its future was in online streaming. While its streaming service continues to grow, DVD subscribers continue to decline. But what sets Netflix apart is the ability to stay ahead of changes that are happening in its industry.[3]

Bear

In 2004 Blockbuster was on top of the world, with 60,000 employees and 8,000 stores. But unlike Netflix, Blockbuster failed to adapt. Almost overnight, no one wanted to go to a video store. More than once, the company had the chance to buy Netflix. Today, there are just 12 stores remaining with Blockbuster franchise agreements.

Bull

Amazon.com started as an online bookseller and has grown to become the largest internet retailer in the world. Many people don't realize it's also the dominant player in cloud-based internet services. Amazon has continued to diversify and invest in future-driven ideas.

Bear

Borders was once a billion dollar bookseller, but it failed to be forward thinking even as customers were quickly changing their buying habits. They outsourced their online sales, didn't develop an e-reader, and neglected e-books in general. Amazon and Barnes & Noble were more responsive to market changes and they capitalized on the move to digital. Borders was forced into bankruptcy when they couldn't attract a buyer for the distressed company.

Bull

Other companies may have products that work just as well, but they don't elicit the passionate feelings consumers have towards Apple. The tech giant has generated an incredible following. People stand in lines for the release of a new iPhone. They keep it simple. Apple doesn't have a large catalog of products. But their products feature simplicity, a sleek design, and a unique customer experience. Steve Jobs once said he would never make a phone. And the rest is history.

Bear

Sony was the Apple of the 80's and 90's. The Walkman was a portable cassette player that revolutionized portable music. Everyone wanted a Walkman. It was the coolest electronics device of its time. Sony transitioned to portable CD players and remained a major player, until 2001 when Apple's Steve Job announced a device that would crush Sony. The iPod became the bestselling device of the 2000's and was the predecessor of the iPhone. Sony was working on its own MP3 player devices, but it never caught up with Apple. Sony was too slow to innovate.

Companies today must be nimble, adaptable, and creative. Some of these companies seem to almost exist in the future. They are ahead of the curve. If Google is 20 years in the future, is it acceptable for schools to be 20 years in the past? Is your school a time capsule or a time machine?

I see some schools really trying to adapt. They are fighting to avoid becoming a time capsule. But there are forces that make it very difficult to change. Other schools aren't really attempting to change much. It's business as usual. And that approach will lead to obsolescence, much like the companies on the bear list. And our *business* as educators is critically important because our bottom line is not measured in dollars but in changed lives.

Cultures of Innovation

If you're changing the world, you're working on important things. You're excited to get up in the morning. —Larry Page, co-founder Google

Google

Google has been the epitome of innovation among the tech giants. Google has 9 principles of innovation that guide the company's culture. Many schools have already borrowed from the Google playbook by developing Genius Hour or 20-percent Time, where students are given time in their schedule to pursue projects they are passionate about.

Google's 20-percent Time has resulted in the development of valuable products like Gmail and Google Earth. Schools should consider utilizing the 20-percent Time framework for both students and teachers. For students, it provides opportunities for self-discovery and high-interest learning. For teachers, the opportunity to pursue side-projects would result in new practices and possibilities. As an added benefit, the greater sense of autonomy would lead to increased motivation and professional satisfaction.

Google is constantly working on new ideas. While business experts and investors called for the company to focus on its profit-driving search engine, Google pursued a different approach. The company relentlessly pursues new ideas and new possibilities.

Many of these ideas are complete failures. But some of the ideas in the pipeline stick. Just look at the education market. Over 20 million students and teachers use Chromebooks at least weekly, and there are over 70 million G Suite for education users. Every student in our school uses a Chromebook daily.

What if schools pursued new ideas and possibilities with a fervor similar to Google? What if we let go of some of our preconceived notions about what works and develop bold audacious approaches. Would some of them fall flat? Sure, but some of them would be home runs. And the culture of our schools would come in line with the culture of change and innovation that is characterizing our era.

Another one of Google's 9 principles is to have a mission that matters. Google has created incredible value for its customers through the development of extremely useful products and services. Google impacts millions of users, including all the students and teachers mentioned before. Plus, its employees drive the mission to continue to create even greater access to information and communication. Google has a mission its employees can fully embrace. They feel like they are making a difference every day.

As educators, schools have a mission that matters most. We are in the business of changing lives and helping kids have better opportunities in life. But all too often, top-down mandates suck the life out of the classroom and educators lose sight of the mission. The ideas that would create the greatest energy for continuous improvement are crowded out by doing stuff in a standardized, prescriptive way. School leaders must focus on clarifying a shared sense of mission that is truly a mission and not focused on test results. And then allow teachers the freedom to create ideas and build on their individual strengths in the classroom. Ultimately, teachers must drive the mission to create the most amazing learning opportunities possible.

Starbucks

Starbucks was built on creating a personalized experience for customers. Sure, coffee is great, and it's great to be able to customize your latte or Frappuccino to your liking. That's part of the magic. Customers love to be creative in exploring unlimited possibilities in the Starbucks menu. But beyond the beverages, the Starbucks culture is focused on connecting with the customer. What really sets the company apart is the ability to provide an experience that connects on a personal level.

Learning is also personal and should not be a one-size-fits-all experience. Schools that are future-focused will aim to provide students with experiences tailored to their needs that allow for voice and choice in learning.

So schools should consider these ideas for being more like Starbucks.

1. Get to know students on a personal level.

2. Give students voice and choice.

3. Provide Wi-Fi, and access to devices.

4. Provide flexible seating and collaborative spaces.

5. Value creativity.

Amazon

Amazon is probably my favorite company. I love the fact I can order online and have my item delivered incredibly fast and well-packaged. And if there is ever a problem, the customer service is incredible. But what can schools learn from Amazon, you're thinking?

Like Google, Amazon has a relentless focus on providing value to its customers. They don't focus on beating competitors or winning market share. Instead, they focus on meeting their customers' needs.

Let's stop trying to beat standardized tests and focus that energy on creating greater value for students and their futures. Amazon has a strong entrepreneurial culture. The company seeks talent that is interested in developing new ideas and encourages idea development from all levels of the organization.

Creative and talented people want to work for Amazon. If schools encouraged this type of culture, perhaps education would retain more of its best and brightest. We need to attract and retain teachers who are passionate about making a difference and who are creative risk-takers.

I'm not sure the culture in most schools supports the needs of these entrepreneurial educators. Amazon always strives to get better. The company has seen incredible growth, and it's considered one of the most admired companies in the world, yet it doesn't rest on its laurels. Schools also need to continue to improve and never be satisfied with the status quo. Always be working to create an even better experience for students.

Zappos

I couldn't resist including Zappos in this list. The internet retailer—mainly known for shoes, fast shipping, and incredible customer service—was included because of their innovative core values.

1. Deliver WOW through service
2. Embrace and drive change
3. Create fun and a little weirdness
4. Be adventurous, creative and open-minded
5. Pursue growth and learning

6. Build open and honest relationships with communication

7. Build a positive team and family spirit

8. Do more with less

9. Be passionate and determined

10. Be humble

The unrelenting focus on providing value to the customer seems to be a common theme among all the companies I've featured. But what sets Zappos apart is the focus on creating a really fun workplace. But schools can learn from this too. I always say we're going to work hard and have fun while getting the job done.

As we are working to re-imagine how school will meet the needs of the future, we should remember to enhance the fun factor. Learning should be fun; let's celebrate a little weirdness, just like Zappos.[4]

Getting a Job or Creating a Job

My great uncle worked for General Motors his entire life. As a young man, he moved his family hundreds of miles to Flint, Michigan to take a factory job that promised security and prosperity. He was loyal to the company and the company was loyal to him. He retired with a nice pension. Today, the hope of getting a middle-class job in a factory is unlikely. Manufacturing is on the decline. Routine and manual labor are under tremendous pressure.

In the past, the typical worker had one job for 30+ years.

Millennials will work a dozen jobs from 18 to 42. They will move from job to job to advance more quickly and find the working environment where their skills fit the best.

And what will the future of work look like?

Instead of getting a job, people will create a job or jobs. They will have multiple streams of income that allow for more autonomy and flexibility than working as an employee. Platforms will continue to develop to match talent with specific projects.

In a few years, up to 40% of the American workforce, about 60 million people, will be independent workers.[5] These freelancers, contractors, and temp workers will even include highly trained professionals like attorneys and marketing experts.

The knowledge economy allows for entrepreneurship in hyperdrive. Your ideas and skills can spread quickly and create incredible value by leveraging networks. But you have to stand out from the crowd. You must be adaptable.

You don't create a job through consumption and compliance. It takes creativity and originality.

Guitars or Hand Grenades

The teacher across the hall had a guitar and a ponytail. He read poetry. His students did creative stuff. He was always connecting, listening, and challenging kids. His advice to me was to teach them how to think. He inspired his students, and he inspired me too.

The other teacher down the hall would look at me between classes and pretend to pull the pin from a hand grenade with his mouth, and then toss it into the hallway. I cringe just writing that last sentence. He constantly complained about how kids weren't as good as they used to be. Again, more cringing.

It's disappointing to think that any teacher would think the solution to their problems is better kids. We can't pick who we teach. We teach them all. They are potential world changers.

The ponytail teacher left education within five years. The system didn't give him a place to thrive. He knew it wasn't all about standards or achievement reports.

But the hand grenade teacher retired after 30 years. Funny, retirement was all he ever talked about.

Who would be attracted to the culture at Google, or Starbucks, or Zappos? The ponytail teacher or the teacher who was counting the days to retirement?

Hired by Google

Google has been referred to as the 'world's most attractive employer.' So what's it take to get hired there? Perfect grades? A degree from an elite university? Top scores on standardized tests?

Lazlo Bock, Google's senior vice president of people operations, revealed that Google finds "G.P.A.'s are worthless as a criteria for hiring, and test scores are worthless... We found that they don't predict anything." Up to 14% of Google employees don't even have a college degree.[6]

So what is most important to Google?

1. The ability to learn.

2. The ability to lead.

Bock clarified that grades don't hurt, but some of the top students don't have the other qualities Google wants in its employees, like the ability to learn.

"If it's a technical role, we assess your coding ability, and half the roles in the company are technical roles. For every job, though, the No. 1 thing we look for is general cognitive ability, and it's not I.Q. It's learning ability. It's the ability to process on the fly. It's the ability to pull together disparate bits of information. We assess that using structured behavioral interviews that we validate to make sure they're predictive."

And the second is "leadership — in particular, emergent leadership as opposed to traditional leadership. Traditional leadership is, were you president of the chess club? Were you vice president of sales? How quickly did you get there? We don't care. What we care about is, when faced with a problem and you're a member of a team, do you, at the appropriate time, step in and lead. And just as critically, do you step back and stop leading, do you let someone else? Because what's critical to be an effective leader in this environment is you have to be willing to relinquish power."

Schools should take note of how Google and other forward-thinking organizations are viewing grades and standardized tests. Clearly, Google wants adaptable learners, employees who demonstrate learning in authentic, unpredictable situations, not just on tests.

And they want humble leaders, who step forward when they have something worthwhile to offer but defer to others' better ideas.

Some of the highest achievers in school have never dealt with failure and lack the humility or flexibility to deal with situations that are complex or uncertain. Being good at traditional school doesn't always translate well to life beyond school.

Creating Innovative Spaces

When you look at some of the most innovative companies, they are encouraging innovative thinking throughout their culture. Even their workplace designs are innovative. They don't create offices that look like the offices of 1965 or even 1985. They design spaces that encourage the type of thinking, interaction, and engagement that is relevant now and for the future.

Earlier I mentioned how the classroom I visited last summer was just like the ones I had when I was in school years ago. The desks were in straight rows. The teacher's desk was at the front of the room. The decor was not relevant to anything happening in the world today.

What message does this send? What type of learning is valued in this space? Tom Murray (@thomascmurray) has referred to desks in rows as the *'cemetery effect'* because of the chilling impact that format has on collaboration and sharing.[7] Desks in rows look like a cemetery. It's the 'death' of learning. Insert ominous music here.

I realize there are good teachers who have desks in straight rows. But we need to consider how our classrooms are reflecting the changes in the world around us. What message are we sending in the setup of the learning space? Does your classroom design show that you value collaboration? Is it teacher-centered? Or, learning-centered? Is it a shared space, where ideas of students and teachers are valued? And where teachers and students are working together to accomplish goals?

Principal Christopher Weis (@ChrisWeissCT) asked his teachers to *not* have their classrooms entirely ready for when students arrived at the beginning of the year.[8] He wanted teachers to work with students to consider some of the design elements of the classroom. Students will feel more invested if they have some input on how the class looks. I think it's great when teachers reveal their personality in the design of the classroom. Why not also ask students to also reveal what they like in adding to the decor?

One of the biggest trends in classrooms is flexible seating and flexible spaces. Flexible seating might include standing desks, exercise balls, benches, etc. Flexible spaces allow for the classroom to be configured for various sizes of collaborative groups. Or, it can be transformed for designing, making, or direct instruction depending on what is needed at the time.

Several teachers in our building get creative with seating choices and spaces. And for the most part, they do it without spending a fortune on expensive furnishings. These classrooms energize students and adults. Goodbye rows that deaden the flow.

We must consider why we are making the design choices for our classrooms and schools. Is my design choice better for me as teacher or principal? Or is it better for students? Is it better for learning?

Extend these questions to everything we do as educators. We aren't teaching students from 20 years ago, so our classrooms shouldn't look like 20 years ago either. And our own comfort is not as important as creating opportunities for students.

I mentioned several of our teachers are working to create modern learning spaces for students. But perhaps the most striking transformation in our school is our library. Before, it was pretty much a traditional library. It was a nice space that was friendly and inviting. But now it is truly a *learning commons*, a place where students gather to share ideas, work on projects, and use technology.

The entire feel is different. It feels like a Starbucks. We even have coffee. There are also lots flexible spaces for collaboration, flat screen T.V.'s, cafe tables, and distinctive lighting. Student design elements and art are on display throughout the space. An adjacent computer lab is now a makerspace complete with a green screen.

A High School Start Up

In our school, we want to create a culture of freedom to teach and make art. We want to be student-driven and future-driven, and support that with standards. But in too many schools, teachers feel like they must ask permission to try something new or take a risk.

But a culture of permission is not going to develop expectations of innovation. I don't want our teachers to feel the need to get permission to try something they believe could impact learning for students. I love it when teachers share the ideas they are trying. I also love to play a part in supporting these ideas.

With six weeks left in the school year, one of our English teachers and her students hatched an idea to create an online literary magazine that would feature writing from students and community members. Anyone in our community was invited to submit their short stories, poetry, and prose to the magazine for publication.

It involved community. It had a mentor. She didn't solve all the problems for them. There was risk of failure and celebration of success. It combined literacy with entrepreneurship. In the end, the students were very proud of what they accomplished in such a short time. And they practiced a whole variety of valuable skills.

Think Tank

You don't have a research and development team to help you innovate.

Or maybe you do?

Your students have amazing ideas and if you activate them as your think tank, they will amaze you with the possibilities they envision. They will need your guidance and wisdom to help them along the way, but when you work in partnership with them, it changes everything. They will take greater ownership of learning than ever before. They will start to care more about creating something worthwhile and meaningful, instead of just wanting to be done.

You can be the difference. When you really listen to your students, you can find ways to inspire them. Abraham Lincoln is credited as saying, "The best way to create the future is to invent it." You can work with your students to create a better future for them. Of course, there will be challenges to overcome. There are structures, mandates, and standardized tests to think about. I realize that.

But even smaller changes can make a huge difference. Think creatively. Bring the best of you to the classroom. When you work together with your students to co-create learning, you move the needle toward a more future-driven classroom. Your leadership makes the difference.

We must create schools that reflect the world we live in, not the one we grew up in. #FutureDriven

So, model change and adaptability for your students. Don't drag your students through a curriculum. Invite them to come along with you for a shared journey of discovery.

They will thank you. The experience will be remarkable and will help move education toward a more adaptable, innovative system. We must create schools that reflect the world we live in, not the one we grew up in.

CHAPTER 4

Connect, Grow, Serve

We rise by lifting others. —Robert Ingersoll

I've always believed relationships were important, but I've also come to realize I'm a bit of an introvert too. So, while I've always valued strong relationships, I know how important it is for me to be intentional in this area. At times, I felt positive feelings about our students and staff, yet I assumed they knew how I felt. I assumed they knew I cared about them and wanted the best for them. I assumed they knew I believed in them and wanted to help them make their dreams come true.

Each teacher and administrator at BHS develop a personal learning plan for the school year. I share more about personal learning plans in chapter 9. This year I decided to focus my personal learning plan on building relationships. I started by reading *Kids Deserve It¹*, by Todd Nesloney (@TechNinjaTodd) and Adam Welcome (@awelcome). The book was awesome for inspiring my efforts to be a better principal in this area. It can be tough to make personal connections with over 800 students in a building. But my focus was clearly set on connecting with more students in more meaningful ways.

One of the things I started doing was greeting students every morning. I was always visible in the mornings before school, but I was usually chatting with adults in the building or checking up on one thing or another. But this year I decided to interact with as many kids as possible first thing in the morning, before school even started.

I start at the back door of the building where bus riders are dropped off in the morning. Then, after the last bus pulls through, I head to the front of the building to greet students coming in the main entrance to our commons. I make eye contact with as many students as possible. I smile and say good morning, have a great day, good to see you, welcome, how are you, or it's a beautiful day. I ask about the game last night or give a compliment. Sometimes I give fist bumps or high fives. I try to lift up every student that walks through our doors.

At first, some students seemed surprised, maybe even a little reserved or withdrawn, when I would greet them. They weren't used to this level of personal attention. But over time, more and more students smiled back and said good morning to me, too. In fact, one of our vendors was coming into our school when I was out doing my morning greeting. He was chatting with me for a few minutes as I continued to greet students. He commented, "I travel to schools all over, and I can't imagine a friendlier group of kids." That means more to me as a principal than any trophy or award our school might win.

But that's not the end of the story.

One day I had some help with my greeting routine. One of our students, Daniel, was already at the bus drop off door. He was holding it open. I didn't think too much of it, but then he started showing up every day. He's always there now ready to help, even before I arrive. He's quiet, so he doesn't say much to the other kids as they come in, but many of the other students will tell him thank you as they walk by.

And I've gotten to know Daniel[2] a little. He is passionate about professional wrestling. He looks forward to watching it on TV each week, and he asks me if I watched it too. I asked him if he knew about Hulk Hogan and Andre the Giant, wrestling heroes from when I was a kid. He just grinned and said he heard of them. I also learned a little about his family, where he lives, and some of his favorite things. I even learned we have 22 buses that drop off students in the morning because Daniel counted them for me.

> ## We never know when a simple conversation with a student might spark something lasting and worthwhile.
> ## #FutureDriven

Isn't it amazing the impact our small actions can make? Just showing up in the morning to greet kids inspired Nathaniel to do the same. Our investment in people has a way of multiplying. Daniel wanted to help out. I think he feels good about holding the door open in the morning. I know I feel better each day I get to see Daniel and hang out with him for a few minutes. We never know when a simple conversation with a student might spark something lasting and worthwhile. Every interaction is an opportunity for relationship building.

People First

Relationships are an important part of helping students become adaptable, life-long learners. I've been asked if technology will replace teachers in the future. I don't believe it will. The social aspects of learning are too important. Teachers inspire students to want to learn by showing how much they care. These connections are so important to developing a strong culture of learning. The teacher-student relationship is sacred.

In the future, technology will continue to play a larger role in our lives. We will rely more and more on the advanced tools that are created. But the human element will remain more important than technology. In fact, the human element will become even more valuable and needed to ensure technology is used properly.

Relationships and technology both matter. So does the order. We must keep relationships at the center of all we do as educators. We are in a people profession.

To effectively prepare students for a complex, uncertain future, we must recognize the critical importance of making people our priority. Strong relationships are the foundation of our ability to lead and have influence. You might have some success as an educator with average relationships, but you will never reach your full potential unless you try to lead with your heart.

More Than Machines

Technology is playing a larger role in our lives. It's happening so fast, we may not even realize all the changes. When I started teaching, I didn't have a cell phone. Lori and I didn't have an internet connection in our home. Now we complain when our internet is occasionally slow and Netflix starts buffering.

All the signs indicate that automation, artificial intelligence, and other advancements are taking over tasks now done by people. Machines can do it more efficiently and less costly than relying on human capital.

But there are some things machines cannot do as well as humans. They can't understand emotions, show love, or provide care and understanding. In the future, the things that make us uniquely human will be increasingly valuable. In a world where we rely more and more on progress and technology, we will need to nurture our humanity. We will crave the human element and value people who can bring us closer. The ability to develop lasting, trusting, human relationships will be essential.

Relationships have always been valuable in education. The teacher and student relationship is sacred in my view. But more than ever, schools need to discuss, teach, and model interpersonal skills. We need more empathy, more understanding, and more kindness than ever before. The future-driven educator will make relationships a top priority.

Fieldwork

Many studies support the idea that positive relationships are essential to better learning. A brighter future for students includes a school focused on a culture of better relationships. These findings are compelling evidence that schools as learning organizations must be caring organizations too. Here are a few highlights:

1. John Hattie found that teacher-student relationships had a .72 effect size on student achievement.[3] Positive relationships have a powerful impact on learning.

2. Allan Allday (University of Kentucky) found that greeting students at the door increased student engagement by 27 percent.[4]

3. "Middle school students who reported high levels of developmental relationship with their teachers were 8 times more likely to stick with challenging tasks, enjoy working hard, and know it is okay to make mistakes when learning, when compared with low levels of student-teacher relationships."[5]

4. According to the Harvard Principal Center, "The most powerful predictor of student achievement is the quality of relationship among the staff."

Dr. Roland Barth writes, "...the nature of the relationships of the adults that inhabit the school has more to do with the school's quality and character and with the accomplishments of its pupils than any other factor."[6]

Rigor, Relevance, Relationships

Here's one of our favorite interview questions we use when hiring a new teacher:

Rigor, Relevance, and Relationships—which of these is most important to you and why?

How would you respond to this question?

Each of these 3 R's are important and essential to learning. That's what makes it a challenging and interesting question. I've been critical of using the word *rigor* sometimes because if you look it up in the dictionary, it basically means arduous or severe. I don't think that's what we intend learning to be. But rigor is important when it describes learning that is challenging and results in deeper thinking.

As for relevance, this quality produces learning that is valuable, learning that matters. We know it's important for learning to be relevant and for teachers to help students see the relevance in learning.

But I believe the most important R in this list is relationships. It's fruitless to demand rigor without first having a strong relationship. It starts with valuing the person over performance.

And your students won't care about relevance unless they believe you care about them as a person first.

Your school's success is largely determined by the quality of relationships in your school. Stronger relationships=Stronger schools. #FutureDriven

So I'm suggesting every future-driven leader reframe the 3 R's. As education leader Jimmy Casas (@casas_jimmy) says, start with Relationships, Relationships, Relationships and go from there.

---

9 Ways to Help Your Students Show Up Well

Every teacher wants students to "show up well" to their classroom. It means students are mentally, physically, emotionally, and otherwise ready to learn. We know that doesn't always happen because life happens. Kids are dealing with real issues and problems and brokenness just like every other person on the planet. Some students have most of their needs met and rarely struggle to show up well. For others, it's a constant battle.

No matter if the challenges are big or small, every student who walks through our doors has a unique story. It's a story that influences their ability to learn. And when we don't seek to understand what's going on in their lives, we are missing an important part of our profession. We aren't just teaching the curriculum. We are teaching kids first, and we must understand their needs.

We also must create environments that help students to show up well, even when all of their basic needs might not be met. A positive school culture can help overcome the challenges a student may face. A positive classroom culture can do the same. If we want to build stronger, more respectful learning communities, invest in the lives of your students and never miss a chance to brighten their day.

To prepare students for their future, help them show up well today.

Every student in your school needs to feel physically and emotionally safe. They need to feel a sense of belonging. They need to feel people care about them as individuals, that they matter, that they have dignity. Every student needs to feel respected and supported. When a school or classroom has a positive culture, it creates a secure feeling so students can be fully present and ready to learn, even when stuff outside of school might be tough.

Here are some ideas everyone can use to help students in your school show up well:

1. Greet students, learn names, give high fives and fist bumps. Say hello to each person you meet in the hallway.

2. Get to know your students as people. Ask them about their hobbies, their weekend, or just about anything. Eat lunch with them.

3. Always protect each student's dignity. Show great care and concern. Give respect even when it's not returned.

4. Notice how your students are feeling. Make it safe for them to express their feelings to you without judgment. Ask them if they are okay? Check on them.

5. Smile. Joke around. Use humor to lighten another person's load. Laughter makes life better and even more bearable.

6. Meet a need. Provide a snack or a jacket or a pencil. If you can't meet the need, find someone who can.

7. Encourage and praise. Use your words to inspire and lift up. See the spark of genius in each student.

8. Have high expectations. You can do it. I believe in you. I've seen you overcome this before. You can do it again.

9. Listen with empathy and try to understand. Approach that hurtful comment, behavior, or action with curiosity to understand the child better.

We all want our students to show up well, and together we can create environments to help them do just that. But we also need to work at showing up well ourselves. Educators are human too, and life can be rough on us as well.

Never neglect your own self-care. The teachers I've met throughout the years are some of the most selfless people I've ever known. But if you aren't taking care of you, it will result in resentment, fatigue, and poor emotional health. Our students need us to show up well, too. So take the time to care for yourself and develop a strong support system for your own well-being.

Making Meaningful Connections

Nicholas Provenzano (@thenerdyteacher) shares three simple strategies he uses to connect with students and build stronger relationships in his classroom.[7]

1. He devotes the "First Five Minutes" of class entirely to connecting with students. He engages them in casual conversation with the sole purpose of building better relationships. He uses the time to find out more about their interests, to learn how their day is going, and to understand what's happening away from school. During this time, he has made stronger connections with students that have allowed him to build trust and offer help and support that wouldn't be possible otherwise.

2. He makes it a point to attend students' extra-curricular activities when possible. Students notice teachers who show up for a ball game or a concert. It also shows parents how much you care. And it's a great chance to interact in an informal setting. He writes, "I never encountered a student who wasn't happy to see a teacher at one of these events."

3. He holds regular office hours before school starting at 7:00 am. His early arrival allows students a place to hang out in the morning. Being available has led to some deep conversations, "I give up time in the morning, but I gain important connections with my students that allow me to not only help them with their problems but also engage them in the classroom."

Say Thank You

A person who feels appreciated will always do more than is expected.

I believe in the power of sending positive handwritten notes to every person on our team. At the start of the school year, I fill out envelopes with the names of each staff member that works at BHS. It helps me to be sure to encourage everyone with a handwritten note at least once during the school year. I write additional notes as occasions arise.

I think these sincere expressions of appreciation are more powerful than any tangible rewards I might give my staff. I hope they encourage each recipient. I know I feel encouraged and grateful for the opportunity to convey my feelings and share a word of encouragement.

This year we also carved time out of our faculty meetings to invite teachers to write notes of appreciation to each other or to students. This idea was inspired by a great post by one of my favorite bloggers, Bill Ferriter (@plugusin).[8]

Calling Coach

I hadn't talked with Coach Radford for nearly 25 years. I wasn't even sure he would remember me since he was only my coach for a short time and it was so long ago. But I decided to call him and share the impact he made on me.

He was the varsity basketball coach, but I wasn't a varsity player. I was just a freshman kid he barely knew. In a matter of months, my family moved away, and I was off playing for a different coach at a different school.

But in the short time I knew Coach Radford, he significantly helped shape the direction of my life. When I decided to come out for the team, I wasn't in shape and wasn't a very good basketball player either. I remember in preseason conditioning, I was ashamed at how badly the other boys just left me in the dust in the sprints.

But Coach Radford didn't see me for what I was, he saw me for what I could become. He constantly encouraged me even though I was just a freshman kid who might not ever help his basketball program succeed. Had it not been for his uplifting words, I would've quit.

I'm grateful he believed in me and made me feel like I could do it. And that small action made me want to coach and teach and help students succeed. As

I considered different career possibilities, my memories of Coach were always very powerful in leading me to be a teacher.

And that's how it is for each of us who work with students. We don't know when a conversation or a situation might help spark in a student something lasting and worthwhile. It often doesn't take grand gestures and heroic interventions to make a difference. It simply means investing in students and taking a genuine interest in their life now and in the future.

I was amazed that Coach remembered me immediately. We chatted about life and our families, and I shared with him how much he meant to me. I thanked him.

And he was so gracious in return. Just like before, he made me feel worthy and successful. He said the phone call meant so much to him. He thanked me over and over.

It really is true that none of us has ever accomplished anything by ourselves. There have always been people who have supported us, encouraged us, and even pushed us toward success. Be sure to thank those people while you can. *It's never a good idea to delay gratitude.*

You Inspire

Many students walk into our classrooms carrying a heavy load.

Lend your strength to a student. You have wisdom and life experiences that can make a difference. You have hope and encouragement. Your words can be life-giving to a student.

I borrowed strength from Coach Radford. I could not do it on my own. But knowing he believed in me made all the difference.

Investing in the life of a child affects a day you may never see. Your positive influence pays into the future. Like Coach Radford, you can change lives.

I've learned that people will forget what you said, people will forget what you did, but people will never forget how you made them feel. –Maya Angelou

Build on Strengths

You can't be effective as an educator if you have a critical spirit. Your strength should never be in pointing out other's weaknesses. Unfortunately, our system is focused too much on what kids can't do. We are constantly figuring out ways to close learning gaps, to remediate, to get everyone to the same standard.

But success is not built on weaknesses, it's built on strengths. That's why Usain Bolt is a sprinter and not a marathoner. It's the reason Mick Jagger is in the rock 'n roll hall of fame, not the country music hall of fame. It's why I'm a school principal, not an orthopedic surgeon. We know how important it is to find strengths and nurture them. Adaptable learners are confident learners. We help students believe in their own possibilities.

Success is built on strengths, not weaknesses.
#FutureDriven

This is true for your teaching also. You don't want to be judged by your weaknesses. You want people to recognize your strengths and believe in your value and worth. Your students want the same thing. So, pour your energies into your strengths as a teacher. And pour your energies into the strengths of your students, too.

When we help students find their strengths and use them for learning, we show them they are valued for who they are. Their confidence soars. And with increased confidence, students will want to learn more.

Feedback

Words have power. They matter. They can change the world. And your words can make a world of difference for a child. Words can lift up or they can tear down. They can energize or paralyze. The can bring hope or cause fear.

Daniel Coyle, author of *The Talent Code*, shared findings from a study by psychologists from Stanford, Yale, and Columbia. In the study, students were assigned essays and given different types of feedback on their writing. One type, resulted in a spectacular change in student effort. Students who received this feedback worked to revise their essays much more than those who didn't receive the feedback.

But the magnitude of the change was almost unbelievable. Students who heard these words raised their effort remarkably, by more than 40%. And what were these powerful words?

> I'm giving you these comments because I have very high expectations and I know that you can reach them. [9]

Words have power. Just a few words can inspire effort and increase performance. That's because they are words that connect, that demonstrate belonging, that signal you're important, that show I believe in you. The words weren't even the actual feedback on the essay, but they reveal the power of human connection.

Words have power. They matter. Your words make a difference.

Teachers Are Gift Givers

One of the greatest gifts you can give is hope.

We all feel like failures sometimes. For some students, school has become a constant reminder of their weaknesses. They need hope more than anything. They need someone to believe in them and help them see the incredible gifts they possess.

Teaching standards without inspiring passion, hope, or empathy might still result in some learning, but it is certainly not an education. If a student masters every standard, but does not have a greater sense of hope, meaning, purpose, and passion, I believe we have failed them. Standards are important. But people are more important, and we must teach students first. We must give the gift of education and the gift of hope.

Hope is contagious. Raise hope and you'll raise engagement, defeat apathy, and inspire learning.

Even on your worst day, you are still some child's best hope. —Larry Bell

Never Give Up

I'm a huge college basketball fan, and I'll never forget the speech Jimmy Valvano gave at the 1993 ESPY awards. The beloved coach was battling a terminal cancer diagnosis, but in the midst of his seemingly hopeless situation, his words were filled with anything but doubt.

Cancer can take away all my physical abilities. It cannot touch my mind, it cannot touch my heart, and it cannot touch my soul. And those things are going to carry on forever.

He also shared that he was starting the Jimmy V Foundation for cancer research, and its motto would be, "Don't give up...don't ever give up."

One of my former superintendents and I used to run together. He was responsible for inspiring me (twisting my arm) to run my first marathon. But one day while we were out running, I was sharing a story about a student and how bad their home life was and how incredibly broken the situation was. And then I said, "It's like he (the kid) doesn't even have a chance (in that environment)."

My friend just looked at me, grinned and said, "Oh yes he does (have a chance)."

The moment stuck with me. I was taken aback by the response. And then I was suddenly reminded of my friend's own story he shared with me about his childhood home. He was raised by a single mom, in poverty, with all kinds of hardships and dysfunction. But his circumstances didn't determine his future. He overcame the difficulties of his childhood to become a successful elementary school teacher, then principal, and later superintendent. He rose to the top of his profession despite having all the odds stacked against him.

He's a great husband and dad, too. You could always see how important his family was to him.

That grin and those words reminded me to never think a kid can't make it or that the odds are just too great. The truth is little miracles happen every day. And those little miracles turn into bigger miracles. A big reason my friend rose above the challenges of his childhood was the support and investment from educators. He had teachers who believed in him.

We can't afford to ever give up on a child. Each kid represents incredible hope and unlimited possibilities. They each have a mind that can learn, a heart that can love, and a soul that is priceless.

Ten Things Every Educator Should Say More Often

Our words matter. Our character matters even more. But if you develop strength of character and always seek to grow, your words and actions will flow from who you are. You've worked hard to become the best version of you.

1. "I believe in you."

One of the most powerful things you can communicate is your belief and confidence in your students and your colleagues for that matter. Sadly, too many students (and adults) struggle to believe in their own worth and ability. Above any curriculum outcome, strive to show students their own worth and genius. Say to your students, "I believe in you. You are capable. You are important."

2. "I won't give up on you."

When things are tough, we all need someone to pick us up and be there for us. You can be that person for your students. Every kid needs an adult to fill the gap, a person who is older and wiser, someone they can borrow strength from until they have more of their own. You can be that person when you tell your students, "I won't give up on you."

> *Every child deserves a champion: an adult who will never give up on them, who understands the power of connection and insists they become the best they can possibly be. —Rita Pearson*

3. "I'm here to help."

I strongly believe leaders are servants too. It doesn't matter what your position is in your school, if you have a desire to help others succeed, you can have great influence and make a huge impact. Clearly, you should stand ready to help each student in your classroom. But the most successful educators are ready to help every student in the building. And they use their influence to make the entire school a better place.

4. "I have time."

Anyone feel pressed for time? Yes! We all do, and that's what makes this phrase so important. There are so many demands on our time we become conditioned to protect against anything taking an extra minute. Principals, protect your teachers' time. They need some margin so they feel like they can help each other or their students or a community cause. You can show what you value when you say, "I have time."

5. "Not yet."

Help your students develop a growth mindset by using these two words. When a student says, "I can't" show them how everything changes when you think "I can't, yet." Instead of putting a grade on that paper filled with mistakes, simply write "not yet" and have your students keep working and revising. Remind your students that the expert in anything was once a beginner. Even Luke Skywalker struggled to become a Jedi. He had the force within him, just like our students have it in themselves to succeed.

6. "Let's work together."

When teachers, and parents, and students, community leaders work together, it is powerful. No one ever accomplished anything completely on their own. Someone else always invested, even when it's not evident. When we build partnerships, everyone benefits. When teachers learn together, it has the power to improve teaching and as a result, improve student learning.

7. "Thank you."

Two simple little words. Say them over and again. Be grateful. Our schools will be a better place. Our world will be a better place.

8. "I'm listening."

Show them you are listening. Lean in. You can learn so much. Students have so much to say, so much to share, and they are waiting for someone to truly listen. Seek to understand and not just to reply. Say "I'm listening. Go on." Ask questions. Show the patience and the empathy you know they need.

9. "What if?"

We need more innovative thinking in classrooms and schools. 'What if' is the language of the dreamers and the disrupters. We don't have to do it the way it's always been done. What if we tried something different?

> *If you aren't willing to ask 'what if' you will have to be willing to settle for 'what is.' —David Culberhouse*

10. "What is best for kids?"

As we make tough decisions, we should always be asking this question. Schools exist to serve students and should do their best to always put the best interest of students first. It's a simple question, but we need to hear it more.

It's too easy for other things to distract us from the most important thing in our schools, serving our students best.

CHAPTER 5

Making Learning Irresistible

The first priority in education is to get children excited about learning. The second is to keep them excited. Everything else will take care of itself. —Jason Elsom

There are too many students who find school boring. You see them at your school too, maybe even in your classroom. They are slumped back or propped up. Tired eyes. They are physically living and breathing but little else reveals thinking not to mention brilliance. But we *know* it's there.

Every child has genius.

These children weren't always this way. In each student who has given up on learning, there was once a kid filled with curiosity, wonder, and awe. I can assume this with some certainty because nearly every preschooler I've encountered is a dynamic learning machine. But somewhere in elementary school, a shift starts to happen. Curiosity gets pushed aside and right answers start to take precedence over the joy of learning.

If we want to create adaptable learners, we have to create school experiences that make learning irresistible. We can't help students learn skills that will give them a brighter future unless they are focused and engaged.

Resist the things that make kids want to resist learning. School doesn't have to be a boring, passive experience. Meet students right where they are instead of expecting them to magically find motivation.

If learning is a top priority, then making learning exciting must be a top priority too.

Pirate Lessons

Provide an uncommon experience for your students and they will reward you with an uncommon effort and attitude. —Dave Burgess

In *Teach Like a Pirate*, Dave Burgess (@burgessdave) offers two questions to raise the bar on making learning irresistible:

1. If your students didn't have to be there, would you be teaching to an empty room?

2. Do you have any lessons that are so amazing you could sell tickets for them? Would students willingly pay to be in your classroom?[1]

How is that even possible? How could they ever be so excited about my classroom that they would be there even if they weren't required? Could I ever have lessons that would be so good that students would buy tickets for them?

Burgess completely reframes his classroom to create experiences that have students on the edge of their seats wondering what will happen next.

Whereas the traditional thinking is to "not smile till Christmas," Burgess is seeking to WOW his students from day one. He is still aiming to set clear expectations that will set the tone for the school year, but the tone he is setting is one of incredible engagement and wonder. He is making learning irresistible.

He notes that he shares his plan for the first days so that his readers can evaluate which if any of the ideas will work for them. He writes, "No content standard matters to me until I have established a safe, supportive, and positive classroom environment I need to successfully teach my students. Any time I spend on the front end of the year to establish this environment is not time wasted. In fact, I know it will pay dividends a hundred times over before the end of the year."

Burgess posts a sign outside his class, "You've heard the stories...are you ready for the experience?!!" He is building a sense of anticipation from the beginning.

He plays music as students enter. On every desk is a can of Play-Doh and on the board in giant letters, "Do NOT open the Play-Doh!" Burgess explains, "It is far more important to create a unique experience for them on the first day than it is to be sure they know how many bathroom passes they will have each semester and when it is okay to use the pencil sharpener."

He tells them his class will be different than any class they've ever attended, and he expects them to get involved with creating the outrageously fun and entertaining experience.

He gives them one main rule: This is a NO-MEANNESS ZONE. If he can't create a completely safe environment, students will not be open to taking risks in the learning experiences that he provides.

Burgess then asks the students to use the Play-Doh to create something that represents themselves. He then engages each student in playful banter about their creation and how it represents them with the goal that everyone leaves feeling successful. Another goal is to learn each student's name as quickly as possible.

At the end of the class period, he says something like, "You don't want to miss tomorrow. Something wild and crazy is going to happen at the beginning of class. You can either be here and see it, or just hear the stories about it when you come back."

I bet that makes them curious enough to want to come back the next day!

Finding Flow

True story. The bell rang and nobody moved.

They were completely focused, totally engrossed. They probably didn't even hear the bell because they were so focused on what they were learning. Amazing, right?

How often are students counting down the minutes of each class? They have their eyes on the clock. They start packing up early, preparing themselves for the transition to the next class. Sometimes they are even lined up at the door, waiting for the bell to ring to move on to the next thing.

But not on this particular occasion. The students were so into what they were learning, the teacher had to remind them it was time to leave. You can work more on this tomorrow. You'll be late for your next class. It's time to go.

How often does this happen in your classroom? How often does the learning in your classroom elicit this kind of passion and commitment? If your classroom is like most, it happens infrequently.

I remember when I was teaching high school English, I would tell my students, "If you work hard all hour, I'll give you the last five minutes to relax and just visit with your friends." That was a terrible idea. I would never do that now. If your students are empowered learners, there won't be enough time to learn. They will want to work on their idea and projects beyond your classroom. Of course, as a young teacher, I was doing the best I could with the information I had at the time.

But the underlying message was that learning is "work" and unpleasant and you need a break, so I'll give you some time later to visit. Let's create conditions where students are disappointed there isn't more time to work on whatever they are learning. As for my promise of social time, my students should've been interacting throughout the whole class. I don't have to reserve time for you to visit. You will be talking with your classmates as part of the process. You will be sharing the amazing things you are learning.

We have all experienced moments of flow. It's during these times that we feel we are completely immersed in what we are doing. We are in the zone. Flow is a mental state where we have intense focus, complete involvement, and enjoy the process entirely. We lose track of time. It can happen in learning, play, work, or a variety of activities. When we find our flow, it probably feels more like play even if it's not. It's amazing what we can accomplish when we feel this sense of full absorption in what we are doing. It's where we find our genius.

It seems obvious to me the classroom full of students that didn't budge when the bell rang was experiencing flow. When I heard this report from one of our teachers, I was thrilled. Let's celebrate! That is so cool. We want this type of learning experience for our students.

But should this be a rare happening? Shouldn't every student experience this type of full engagement, at least on a semi-regular basis?

While it's likely not possible to maintain flow at all times, shouldn't it be something we seek to help our students achieve often? Why isn't this a priority? Shouldn't we aim for this type of full engagement? Wouldn't our students be stronger learners now and in the future if they knew the feeling of complete immersion in what they are learning?

But instead, we settle for on-task. If students appear engaged and participate in the lesson, we have achieved success. Or we hear demand for more rigor. That communicates a positive outlook on learning. Rigor does not sound fun. It sounds just a little painful.

So in the name of rigor, we feel the need to assign homework as sighs and groans echo around the room. I'm calling for a culture where students are so excited about what they are learning, they want to extend the learning on their own. They give themselves their own homework because they are curious and what they are learning is interesting to them.

So what are we afraid of? Why are we covering content and teaching lessons without aiming for more? What teacher wouldn't want a classroom full of students who are so into what they are learning, they don't want to stop?

We can have amazing learning that can work for all kids, and we don't have to wait for someone else to change.
#FutureDriven

Maybe we are afraid to give up some control. Maybe we're afraid we won't be the purveyors of knowledge? Or that we won't cover as much curriculum? That students won't be prepared for standardized tests? Or that it just won't work for these kids? Blame, blame, blame. We blame the system. We blame the parents. We blame everyone possible, and just continue to play school and make sure we are good enough.

But it's time to stop playing the blame game. We can have amazing learning that can work for all kids, and we don't have to wait for someone else to change. There are places where this is happening now, even in schools that are quite traditional. What it takes is an innovative teacher.

It takes you. You can create more and more experiences of flow in your classroom. You can make learning irresistible.

But it does require sacrifice. You have to choose different priorities. The first priority is to really know your students and what excites them. It's about relationships. The second priority is to see them fully engaged, and finding moments of flow, as often as possible. And then, your curriculum becomes the third priority. I realize the curriculum is important, but if you have great relationships and a culture of learning, students will exceed your goals for the curriculum.

9 Valuable Ways to Make Learning Irresistible

1. Learning involves choice. Learners need greater ownership and opportunities to make choices regarding time, place, path, and pace.

2. Learning involves student conversations. Whoever is doing the talking is doing the learning.

3. Learning involves creating. Creativity is one of the best ways to find flow.

4. Learning makes a difference. When learning is making a difference for me, for others, or for my community, it matters so much more.

5. Learning involves play. Play involves fun, laughter, imagination. These are great ways to find flow. Making learning a game can be a great way to make learning irresistible.

6. Learning is filled with discovery. Constructivist learning promotes true understanding and appeals to a learner's sense of wonder and curiosity.

7. Learning involves community. Connect with experts. Invite the community in. Go out into the community. Break down the classroom walls.

8. Learning is visible to real audiences. Learning is more relevant and meaningful when I know my work will be valuable to an authentic audience.

9. Learning is challenging. Why can a teen spend hours trying to conquer a video game? That's challenging. And that involves flow. Capture this in the classroom and watch it transform the culture of learning.

Finish Strong

The beginning and ending of each lesson are extremely important to making learning irresistible. If you fail to capture your student's interest and engagement at the very start, you may never get them back. You may not have a second chance to get their full attention to the learning at hand.

And on the other side of the lesson, if you don't plan a strong closing, you may lose the learning you've aimed for so carefully. Endings should cause reflection, bring ideas to closure, and solidify the main points of the lesson. A strong ending will stick with the student and help drive home learning. It will also provide feedback to the teacher about how students are progressing. It will include checks for understanding.

In an article for the blog Edutopia, Brian Sztabnik (@TalksWTeachers) shared several ideas for the most important 8 minutes of a lesson, the 4 minutes at the beginning and ending.[2]

Beginnings

1. YouTube can be a great anticipatory set for just about any lesson on any topic. Showing the right YouTube video can capture students attention right away. Sztabnik shared how he had students draw comparisons between Carl Sandburg's poem *Chicago* and a Chrysler Super Bowl commercial featuring Eminem.

2. Sharing good news is a great way to start class. Start with celebrations to set a positive tone for your class. Several of our teachers have used a gratitude routine with students. Share 3 things you're thankful for from the last 24 hours and try not to repeat something you've been thankful for in the past. It's a great way to be thankful for the little things in life.

3. The opening of class is a great time to use interdisciplinary approaches. Sztabnik writes, "Toss a football around class before you teach the physics of a Peyton Manning spiral. Play a song that makes

a classical allusion for your mythology unit. Measure the angles of a Picasso painting in math class."

4. Write for five minutes about an essential question related to the unit. Students need to write regularly.

Endings

1. Students love to play games. In fact, they will sometimes spend hours working to level-up in a video game. Use that same tactic for learning. Have students chart their progress toward goals, and then establish levels to strive for like beginner, heroic, legendary, and mythic.

2. Exit tickets are a great way to finish a lesson strong. And they can be used in a variety of ways. Robert Marzano describes how they can be used to collect formative assessment data, for student self-analysis, for instructional strategy feedback, and for open communication.

3. Challenge students to compose a tweet or social media post, or find an image that best reflects the learning of the day. It's not necessary to actually post these to social media. Just having students think about their learning through this lens makes it more relevant to their world.

4. Have students write on a Post-it note one thing they learned from someone else in the class. They can stick these on the whiteboard on the way out of class. The next day, start class by reading some of the notes. This activity demonstrates to students how important it is to learn from each other. It's great for building a stronger culture of learning.

What's Your High Score?

The idea of student mastery has driven too much of the discussion recently in education. Mantras emerged like "every kid, every standard" meaning that every student should master every grade level standard.

At one point, early in my admin career, I identified students who were right on the bubble for attaining proficiency, and I directed teachers to give them extra time and support, and it was all part of playing a game to try to make our numbers look better. Schools shouldn't be focused on looking good. They should focus on being good. Actually, they should focus on being great.

But being great is not about having a school with the highest test scores. Being great is showing kids and families how committed we are to kids and learning. Being great is investing in people. When we are doing all we can to help every child succeed, we are an excellent school.

Looking back, I'm ashamed I was playing the test score game. We were investing more energy into kids who were nearing proficiency. We wanted to look good on state assessments. We were allowing scores to define our identity as a school. Of course, we were still teaching all of the kids, but certain students were getting something extra because it was going to help the school's image.

The truth of the matter is that proficiency is not an authentic mission for learning. Our mission is more than a number. If standardized test scores are your school's top priority, then your mission is more about adults than it is about kids. We need to reflect on this and keep the focus on learning.

I'm very competitive. I remember as a kid, I loved the arcade game Galaga. The game was simple, especially compared to today's complex games. You basically controlled a starfighter with the objective of shooting a swarm of aliens. I was a child of the 80's so I spent my fair share of time in arcades. I focused most of my energy on this game. I wanted to be the best at it. I wanted to get the high score, and usually, I did. I played it over and over again.

But now I don't remember how many points I scored or even how many times I got the high score. The meaning behind the numbers faded over time. What I do remember is how much I loved that game. I remember how hard I "worked" to get better at it. It reminds me of my childhood. It helps me relate to my sons, and how much they love video games. Those are the things that matter.

We want students to love learning, not because they are better than someone else or have a higher score, but because it helps them reach their potential and discover who they want to be. Learning provides hope and a better future.

Passion vs. Proficiency

Most schools now are obsessed with proficiency. It's been drilled into the DNA by the past couple of decades of high-stakes standardized tests. And the thing is proficiency isn't bad. It just isn't the only thing. In the current system, your school is good or not so good based on the percentage of students who are proficient in mastering standards.

But proficiency won't make you successful. Knowing your stuff is just a start. And the curious thing is many of the same people sounding alarms about proficiency probably didn't score all that great on standardized tests themselves. I'm calling you out! Maybe along with tax returns, we should demand to see politicians' ACT scores!

More than proficiency, we need passion. We need people who are passionate about life, solving problems, helping others, and doing amazing work. Passionate people aren't just concerned with what's in it for them. They don't want someone to take care of them, to create a job for them, or make it easy for them. They want to make a difference in the world. They want their life to count.

**If our students master every standard
but do not discover joy and passion
in learning, we have failed them.
#FutureDriven**

Proficiency is about cheap labor, following the rules, being an interchangeable part. It's following the map, taking orders, playing it safe. In school, it's being ready for the next grade level or for college. These aren't bad things. But it's not what allows us to use all of our gifts.

Passion is what you bring that is uniquely you. It's fully human. It's creative. It's how you interact and connect. It's you as an artist. Not necessarily the kind that paints or recites poetry. But it's *your* art.

There are teachers who know their content, have great strategies, and work hard every day, and yet they don't get extraordinary results. They are following a formula. They haven't found their voice. They lack passion for their work. They're trying to do a job instead of trying to be an inspiration.

Our students need to be inspired. They need to find passion in their schooling. If students master every standard and do not discover the joy and passion of learning, we have failed them. It's not enough to be proficient. Students need to be passionate and proficient. Both matter. And so does the order. Start with passion and then, proficiency won't be a great struggle.

The Whole Child

Some of the most important lessons learned in school are not related to academics. And they can't be measured on a test.

We can't ignore measures of academic success. But we must also recognize the things that are hardest to measure are often the most important. An education should build character, leadership, and teamwork.

Don't just create lessons for your students. Create experiences. Students will forget a lesson, but an experience will have lasting value. We want to do more than cover content. We want to inspire learning.

And that means we want students to be more excited about learning when they leave us than when they came.

We don't just want them to be better students. We want them to be better people.

We don't just want a high test score. We want to see diligence, courage, compassion, leadership, resilience, creativity, and enthusiasm.

We want students who are not just ready for the future, but who are inspired to create a brighter future and a better world.

When thinking about what kind of learning we ought to have, we should also think about the kind of place we would like the world to be. The next generation of leaders is in our classrooms.

Some people think the purpose of school is academics. *I think the purpose of school is to use academics to unleash human potential.*

Ignite Engagement

I think the shift of agency to the learner is one of our most pressing issues in education. The old ways won't work in an age of instant information and never-ending possibilities for learning. Students (and the rest of us too) are conditioned to expect customization in many areas of life. No wonder they don't respond well to everyone in class learning exactly the same thing on the same day and in the same way.

Yet, school is mostly a standardized experience. If we want students to go all in for learning, we are going to need to empower them to take greater ownership of the experience. We need to make them partners in learning, not just passive receivers of content.

We shouldn't expect kids to learn the way we teach, at least not all the time. We should strive to teach the way they learn. That involves really listening to them and letting them have more choice about what they learn and how they learn it. It also involves helping them find their passions and strengths and then fanning the flame. Great teachers don't just cover content, they inspire learning. How often are students so excited about what they are learning in your class that they want to learn more about it on their own time?

Last year, I asked both our daughters what they were planning to read over summer break. In typical fashion, my oldest daughter Maddie resisted, "Dad, summer is our break from school. Why would I want to spend my summer reading?" Perfect response for a principal's daughter don't you think? Keep in mind she is an excellent student. But nonetheless, I don't think she picked up a book all summer.

But then something changed when she went back to school in the fall. I noticed she was bringing books home to read in her spare time. There were times she would get lost in a book and read for hours. This past December she had books on her Christmas wish list. Of course, we bought them all. She read most of them before Christmas break ended. I was amazed!

Something had happened that was more valuable to me than the content of English class. My daughter's teacher had inspired her to love reading again. When she was in elementary school, she was a reading machine, but somewhere along the way, the joy was lost. But now it was back! Her teacher had a classroom library full of high-interest reading for teens. She didn't force reading on the students, but she modeled it, talked about it, encouraged it, expected it, and constantly fanned the flame. She may not have forced them to read, but she was a force that caused them to want to read!

Our teachers have committed to inspire each of our students to find an identity as a reader. For me, this will always be more valuable than the content covered in English class. If students view themselves as readers, it will enrich their lives in unimaginable ways. They may forget literary terms or vocabulary words, but they will carry the love of reading into their adult lives.

Great teachers don't just cover content, they inspire learning. They create an influence that outlasts them. It carries forward to the next class and ultimately to life.

I think most teachers are extremely focused on how well their students are learning the curriculum over how much excitement students have for learning the subject. Both are important. But if we neglect excitement in learning, we are doing students a disservice. If we create excitement and tap into curiosity, they will likely be inspired to continue learning beyond the school day and beyond the school year.

**Great teachers don't just cover content,
they inspire learning.
#FutureDriven**

CHAPTER 6

Curiosity, Creativity, Risk Taking

The cure for boredom is curiosity. There is no cure for curiosity.
—Dorothy Parker

A few years ago, my son Cooper and I took a trip to Chicago. We drove to St. Louis, jumped on Amtrak and took the train up to the Windy City. It was a three-day trip filled with adventures and amazing food. I wouldn't trade those memories for anything.

Chicago has great museums—The Field Museum, Art Institute of Chicago, Museum of Science and Industry, and more. Cooper and I were especially captivated with the Museum of Science and Industry. If curiosity was like caffeine, this would be your double shot red eye. We were blown away by the interactive displays and filled with wonder and awe at all the amazing sights and sounds. We were both having a blast, and we were learning at every turn.

I remember thinking how different learning was here at the museum than at school. We felt completely free to explore, to experiment, to ask questions, to discuss, and to share new ideas. We were in charge of our own learning. No one was pushing us to learn more. There were no grades or assessments. But we were highly motivated to learn. This place was an amazing environment for generating curiosity. While at the museum, I came across the following quote:

There is no learning without having to pose a question. —Richard Feynman, Physicist and Nobel Laureate

When we are curious, we have questions. And when we have questions, we learn. What if schools created learning opportunities like what can be experienced at a museum? What if we tapped into curiosity? What if instead of pushing students through a curriculum, we also allowed opportunities to investigate and explore? For that type of learning to occur, we must think deeply about how curiosity, creativity, and risk-taking can be increased in schools.

A Curious Mind

Being future-driven is also being curiosity-driven. In a world that is rapidly changing, complex, and uncertain, curiosity becomes paramount. We cannot rely only on what we already know. Making assumptions, believing we know enough is a terrible mistake.

Curiosity helps drive authentic learning. And continual learning is key to adaptability.

Have you ever known someone who asks a lot of questions? Maybe every 4-year-old you've ever met? Children ask amazing questions. Profound, mysterious questions that demonstrate incredible wonder and awe.

But somewhere along the way, we tend to lose our childlike ability to question. Unfortunately, I think school plays a part in this retreat from curiosity. In school, teachers are asking most of the questions. Everyone is expected to learn the same things at the same time. There isn't room for the inconvenience of every child's questions. And that's a shame.

We need to find ways to keep curiosity alive and well. Curiosity is exercise for the mind. It strengthens the brain and causes thinking to be active and not passive. It opens new possibilities and allows for better ideas. And it creates excitement and adventure about the world around us.

Learning Lasts Forever

The word *student* is tainted. It's been twisted, maligned, and terribly undone. Sadly, we have allowed this to happen over years and years of uninspiring experiences in schools. For many, thoughts of being a student are tied to boredom.

Being a student equals lack of freedom. It's about getting by, just finishing, doing what you're told, and making a teacher happy. Few think of the word student and connect it with excitement, energy, and enthusiasm.

And that is why, when I want to use more precise language, I use *learner* to describe the active, engaged, curious, creative, energized *student;* unfortunately many don't associate those qualities with the word *student.*

Besides, being a student is temporary, at least in the formal sense. Kids "graduate" from preschool, kindergarten, elementary, middle, and high school. Some go on to college and graduate again. Even fewer graduate from graduate school. But eventually, being a student comes to an end. It only lasts for a time, while you are in school. But learning lasts forever. Never stop learning.

You see, learning is for life, not just the next grade level.

We aren't *just* preparing kids for college or career, or even the next grade level. Ultimately, we are preparing them for life. We want them to be lifelong learners. We want them to rediscover and hold on to that curious mind they had as a young child. We want them to continue learning beyond their formal education.

Our goal should be for kids to be more excited about learning tomorrow than they are today. To me, that is more important than any test score. It is the most important outcome. It's the ultimate skill. It's learning how to learn. It's the only way to ensure we are creating adaptable learners who can transfer skills from school to life. It's the only way to succeed in the face of an unpredictable and uncertain future.

The Elixir of Learning

Curiosity is inconvenient. It's messy. It leads to questions. It gets you in trouble.

But curiosity matters. It leads to deeper learning.

It's an amazing adaptive skill. It observes its surroundings. It notices what is unusual, uncommon, and marvelous. Humans are hardwired for curiosity. And yet our classrooms emphasize covering content and mastering standards over any consideration of this essential aspect of learning.

Curiosity is where the magic happens. It's the elusive elixir. It's what turns passive students into active learners. The philosopher's stone is a legendary substance sought after by alchemists. It was believed to be capable of turning base metals like mercury into precious gold. Like the Holy Grail, a Masonic keystone, or the fountain of youth, the ancients went on quests to obtain its power.

And likewise, educators must be on a quest to preserve, promote, and unleash the power of curiosity. It's like gold. It's precious to learning. And we know it's not mythical. And perhaps it's not all that elusive. There it is, right under the surface. It's in every student. It's just waiting to be awakened. It's waiting to spark.

And every educator can provide that spark. You can be that inspiration. Model curiosity. Students learn so much from observing behaviors around them. Are you plowing through a curriculum or are you asking interesting questions and learning right alongside your students? How often do you ask questions fueled by your own curiosity, "What if...?" or "Why not...?" or "I wonder...?"

Cause Curiosity

The whole art of teaching is only the art of awakening the natural curiosity of young minds for the purpose of satisfying it afterwards. —Anatole France

Students should be more excited about learning when they leave us than when they arrive. That must be one of the chief aims of education. Kindergarten students are filled with curiosity. Let's make sure they are still curious as 5th graders, as 9th graders, and when they walk across the stage at graduation. Let's keep them excited about learning!

But how do we do that? That's a key part of what every teacher should think about in developing learning experiences for students. That's where you can bring your talents and gifts to your work. You can leverage your skills and your artistry in the classroom. Your personal touch is invaluable as you lead learning with your students. You must live out your own curiosity in your work!

No one can give you a list that will automatically increase curiosity in your classroom, but I'm going to try. Seriously, inspiring learning is about investing yourself in your students. It's a gift you develop and offer. You will get better at creating a climate of curiosity only through consistent practice and ongoing efforts. But it can be helpful to have some ideas on where to start.

1. Learn student interests
2. Create mystery
3. Have students develop their own questions
4. Allow students to explore, tinker, and make
5. Develop passion projects
6. Add intrigue to your classroom decor
7. Integrate art into core subjects
8. Create a student edcamp
9. Take risks

Push, Produce, Practice, Publish

Opportunity is missed by many because it wears overalls and looks like work. —Thomas Edison

Creativity is an expression of curiosity. When we are curious about the world around us, it leads us to more creativity and better ideas. But not every idea we have is a good one. Not every curious thought is going to lead to an interesting question or a discovery that really sticks with us. The key to having great ideas and developing powerful learning moments is to have lots of ideas and moments. Some of them will be great and some of them will fall flat.

I think classrooms have too many boring routines that require very little of students in terms of thinking, creating, and producing. Students are conditioned to a status quo experience that requires very little from them. They aren't producing enough volume of work to really discover the amazing thoughts and ideas buried inside them.

So when teachers want to try something creative or seek to give students work that empowers, they are faced with resistance. Students say, "I'm just not creative" or "I can't think of anything." or "I don't have any good ideas." Creativity is not routine in their experience. They haven't been required to think, produce, and publish.

We must push students out of this learned helplessness. Teachers must take risks in the classroom, constantly. Teachers must model producing and publishing their own ideas and require this from their students too.

Creative people aren't just born creative. They produce lots of work and some of it is awesome. Some of it not as awesome. But they are putting themselves out there—the best they can offer. They are creating something and sharing it with others. It requires practice.

Here are some exercises for practicing curiosity and creativity in your classroom. Future driven educators are constantly talking about how important creativity is, but too many aren't sure where to start. These activities will help students get accustomed to creative thinking in the classroom.

1. Design a personality sandwich. Have students create a personal sandwich that reflects their personality. It's a great activity to get to know each other better. What ingredients would you include on the sandwich and how does that reflect who you are?

2. Ask students to develop a list of possible reasons why the standard pencil color is yellow. Give them a specific number to shoot for—10, 15, or 20 reasons. When you ask them to generate a volume of ideas, you will get better ideas.

3. Show students an everyday item and ask them to think of other ways the item might be used. Repurposing items can require creative thinking and have practical value. What are 10 ways to use a fishing pole beside for fishing? The same thing could be done with a paperclip, an old car tire, a brick, or a worn-out pair of jeans.

4. Give students a paper with lots of small circles and squares printed on it. Ask them to use each of the circles and squares to create a drawing of something, anything. Each circle or square must become something unique. The first ideas might be a smiley face or a snowman, but they will develop more creative solutions as they are forced to develop lots of these drawings.

5. Six word stories are great for developing creativity. Can you write an entire story in six words? You bet. We did this activity with our staff as a team builder and because what we ask of teachers often transfers to what they ask of students. Lots of examples can be found at http://www.sixword-stories.net/.

6. Force connections between unlike items. So much creativity involves finding connections between things that might not seem related at all. That is the beauty of a metaphor, right? So, show students a banana and a baby blanket, and ask for how they might be connected or similar. Again, asking them to think of 10 ways will result in more unusual similarities and more distinct, creative ideas.

7. Solve a problem using superhero alter egos. Childhood obesity is a growing problem in our country. How would Batman address the problem? What would Spiderman do about it?

8. Try an anti-logic simulation. Think about how a person might react to a typical problem. What would be a completely different reaction and what might the outcomes be? For instance, if I was feeling sick to my stomach, conventional wisdom might be to rest, eat only bland foods, or maybe sip on a cold Sprite. But what if my solution was to head to a Mexican buffet, slam some energy drinks, and ride a roller coaster? What might the outcomes be? Your middle schoolers would like thinking about that one I bet. They can create their own scenarios too.

9. Try some brain writing. Have students write a quick solution to a problem you present. They pass on to the next person in the group who adds to their idea for a solution with no cross talk.

10. Have students think about swapping kinds of systems. So you are applying some type of system to a new context. A vacuum cleaner is a type of system used to help keep our carpets clean. What if we applied this system to school? To help curb tardies. To handle bullying. To address boredom.

11. Have students write a letter *without* using I, me, mine, my. It's a challenge!

12. Have students observe surroundings in detail. You might take them outside or to a different area of the school to do this.

13. Teach students about Sketchnoting. Instead of plain old written notes, Sketchnoting involves creating a visual representation of your thoughts as you listen to a speaker or read a book. It relies on the imagination and stimulates creativity.

These are simple ideas to practice creative thinking. With some adaptations, you might be able to tie them more closely to your content standards. But even if you can't think of ways to do that, they are good for helping to create a culture of curiosity and creativity in your classroom.

As your students get accustomed to this as a normal part of your classroom, they will get more comfortable using their own creative abilities.

Synergy

It's impossible to fulfill the potential for creativity and curiosity in learners without also developing collaboration in learning spaces. True collaboration causes a kind of synergy that multiplies the talents, ideas, and understandings of individuals. The smartest person in the group becomes the group.

Collaboration improves ideas. Great ideas improve when shared. Sharing ideas generates new ideas and creates opportunities for combining ideas in creative and curious ways.

Collaboration is built on the social construct of learning. We learn best when we work together. It makes for stronger relationships and helps connect learning and people.

Collaboration challenges our thinking. Truly opening ourselves to other perspectives is a necessity for a mature thinker. When we collaborate, we get beyond how we experience an idea and understand it from another person's viewpoint.

Collaboration helps students learn to seek and give help.

Collaboration is teamwork. Although specific tasks might be completed by individuals, planning and input come from the team. The individual strengths of team members are leveraged for the good of the team.

Collaboration goes beyond cooperation. It involves shared purpose, shared work, interdependence, and trust. That last one deserves repeating. There must be trust.

Collaboration and conflict can and should coexist. Divergent thinking should be encouraged and expressed. But so should resolving conflict and finding shared meaning.

Collaboration is a future-driven skill. In order to be adaptable in a world of rapid change, we must be willing to work together to solve problems and uncover possibilities.

Collaboration is built on a foundation of trust.
#FutureDriven

Okay, okay...I understand why this is important, but I can't get my students to collaborate! I've tried, and it's been a complete failure. My students don't have the social skills to make this work.

You're not alone! It can be challenging to develop authentic teamwork among students. It requires patience and persistence on the part of the teacher. Here are a few tips to consider for improving collaboration.

1. Teamwork requires practice. As students have more opportunities to collaborate, they develop stronger skills for effectively working together.

2. Teams need consistent feedback from the teacher and from each other to improve. It's important to pause and reflect on how teams are functioning.

3. Empathy is critical to effective collaboration. Team members must treat each other with respect and build on that to develop trusting relationships. Teach your students why empathy is important to good teamwork.

4. Use structures to help guide what happens in teams, especially at the beginning of a project. Before teams start to make decisions and assign responsibilities, start with team activities that are teacher directed.

5. When you feel they are ready, give teams complex problems to solve. Real collaboration hinges on the complexity of problems teams are solving. There is no reason to collaborate if the task could just as easily be solved by team members working independently. We want to move students beyond 'divide and conquer' thinking. We want them to have to make critical decisions together.

Awe and Whimsy

If we are serious about increasing curiosity and creativity in our classroom, one key is to not take ourselves too seriously. If you bring energy, excitement, and the unexpected to your lessons, you might find the students are more curious and creative, too. Teachers must model the same risk taking they want to see from students as learners. As Will Rogers proclaimed, "Sometimes you have to go out on a limb because that's where the fruit is."

Once when I was still coaching, we were in a very important tournament and facing one of the best teams in the state from a class larger than us. I knew they were going to be tough to beat. So for my pregame speech, I decided to take a big risk. I was going to do something so crazy and unexpected that it would, hopefully, motivate the team and take away some of their nerves.

I went into my speech about our opponent and how they were pretty good, and we were going to have to play our best game to beat them. And that there would probably be times we would want to give up, but we had to be the ones who didn't flinch. We couldn't let them get the best of us.

I had brought along a large bucket that I prepared upon arrival at the gym by filling it with water. It was sitting on a small table in front of me as I delivered the opening to my speech. I'm sure the players wondered why it was there.

And then I explained, "I'm going to show you what it means to push through even when things get tough. I'm going to stick my head in this bucket of water and hold my breath for as long as I possibly can. And the whole time, I'm going to think about why I started. I'm going to focus on how bad I want to do my best, to stretch myself, to test my limits."

Now I realize there is a distinct difference between weird and whimsy. And right now, you may be thinking I'm weird. But that's okay. Stay with me.

The girls on the team stared in utter disbelief at what they were seeing. But they definitely weren't bored. Engagement was high at this point in the lesson!

And then my head went under. And I stayed under. And I stayed under some more. Until I couldn't take it anymore.

I came up gasping for air, paused to regain my senses, and then, with my arms flailing wildly, exclaimed, "Now go out there and play your best game yet." We all put our hands together in the huddle. You could see the electricity in their eyes. Some were grinning, maybe even giggling a little, but they were ready to play, and I knew it had worked.

We went on to win by the narrowest of margins. It was probably our best win of the entire season, and we won 25 games that year.

Teachers must model the same risk taking they want to see from students as learners. #FutureDriven

In our classrooms, we have lost a sense of whimsy about learning. It should be fun and exciting. It should challenge us to reach higher and do more. It helps our fears melt away. It helps us believe in our possibilities. It should never be mundane or boring or predictable.

Now you may be thinking that life doesn't always work that way. Sometimes we have to just do boring stuff, and kids need to learn to do stuff that isn't always exciting. You may be thinking that you're not an entertainer, you're a teacher, right? I've heard this before, "Kids nowadays want to be entertained all the time. They want instant gratification."

But I don't think life has to be mundane and boring. My wife and I are traveling and staying in a hotel as I write this. This morning at breakfast one of the guys working there was joking around with us and having a good time.

You could tell he was really enjoying his job. He was making it fun. He could just as easily be putting in his time and hating life. But instead, he was busy putting a smile on our faces.

The people who really make life better for all of us know how to take even the mundane and boring parts of life and make them wonderful. It's not about being an entertainer. Some of us aren't entertainers. But we can all look for the whimsy in what we do. We can ask our students to partner with us in making learning fun. Ask them to help you.

We ultimately want exactly the same things our students want. It's two things. We want community (fun, whimsy) in the classroom. And, we want learning (curiosity, creativity) in the classroom. Yes, your students may not always act like they want either, but they do. You just have to help them get past all the defenses they've built to self-protect. School (and life) hasn't always felt safe to all of them.

Here are some questions to consider related to bringing whimsy to your classroom:

1. Would you want to be a student in your own classroom?

2. "If your students didn't have to be there, would you be teaching to an empty room?" —Dave Burgess

3. Do you ask your students about how things are going in your classroom, from their perspective? Not to find out if you're a good teacher or not. But out of curiosity of how they feel and how that information might help you make better decisions for them.

4. What are ways you can bring more whimsy into your classroom? In my example, I was doing something completely crazy that might be totally out of character for you. I would still challenge you to do it anyway. But there are also things related to how you design your lessons that can be whimsical and awe-inspiring.

Not Just for the Arts

I am a big believer in fine arts as an essential part of schooling. The fine arts are incredibly valuable on their own merits, but they also develop skills that transfer to success in a complex, increasingly unpredictable world. Creativity is not just for the arts. Creativity is needed in every discipline, in every field.

It's important to recognize there are different kinds of creativity. Creative people are not just artists, poets, and musicians. Creativity is also helpful in science, math, business and more. All sorts of critical thinking, like solving problems, birthing new ideas, and discovering possibilities, show creativity.

Unfortunately, I think most people have too narrow a definition of creativity.

Creativity Involves Taking Risks

Only those who dare to fail greatly can ever achieve greatly. —Robert F. Kennedy

School has traditionally rewarded conformity over originality. The traditional school works well for some students. Those who conform. But some of our best divergent thinkers don't play the game of school. We need to encourage more diversified thinking.

Many of the most spectacularly successful people were not particularly successful in school. Playing it safe and fitting in might be a formula for school success, but it is not the way to make the biggest impact in life.

Creative thinking requires a willingness to take a risk. It doesn't necessarily have to be a huge risk, but it requires risk. In fact, risk is an important part of all learning. We learn by mistakes. But in the typical classroom, right answers are highly valued over revealing the thinking of students who are still learning. As a result, the idea of practicing and maybe not succeeding right away doesn't seem like a safe thing to do. It's easier to completely disengage than to risk not having the right answer right away.

Of course, not every risk is healthy. We need to use risks to pursue our dreams, help others, and reach for our potential. We should never take risks to escape our pain or be dishonest with ourselves. Some risks are harmful and lead to addiction or self-destructive behaviors.

At the end of life, most people regret the risks they didn't take more than the ones they did. We learn so much from doing things that really challenge us. Our schools and classrooms need to be places where risk is encouraged and failure is part of the learning experience.

Why Don't We Teach Every Child Like They Are Gifted?

The curriculum in any quality gifted program emphasizes creativity, curiosity, critical thinking, and social/emotional skills. These skills are believed to be very important in helping gifted students reach their potential.

Our youngest son, Cooper, was in our school's gifted program. Actually, all of our kids are gifted in a variety of ways, but he met the criteria established to qualify for the program. As a result of his inclusion in this program, he had opportunities to do amazing projects, perform plays, attend space camp, and get extra support with social and emotional aspects of life. In his gifted classes, it always seemed content knowledge was secondary to creativity, critical thinking, and problem-solving. Learning was designed to be an experience and not just a standard or objective to check off the list.

So why don't we teach every child like they are gifted? The question is especially relevant if you believe every student is gifted, even if they are not identified as a gifted student by a test. All students have unique needs, but all students need to experience awe and wonder in learning.

White Space

We need to increase creativity and personal meaning for everyone involved in education--teachers, students, administrators, etc. Creativity results in greater meaning and more personal relevance. It results in more perseverance. It results in positive change. It turns schools into learning organizations instead of information organizations.

But too often, leaders want to get behind people and push them toward an outcome. We develop one-size-fits-all programs. We hold never ending trainings. We mandate this or demand that. We pile on more paperwork.

It's piled on from every level of our system. What's next is coming at us from federal, state, local, and building levels.

We even require a lot of the new stuff in the name of change. We need to change this or that. We need more technology integration. Everyone must use this new method or strategy.

And this crazy dance goes on whether it works or not.

But what if there is another way? What if we provided more white space to allow professionals to develop their own ideas, to start their own movements, to share more of who they are and what they believe in as educators?

Instead of pushing, maybe just a nudge is all that's needed.

A nudge that encourages, "You have great ideas. You should share that."

A nudge that challenges, "How could we give students more ownership in that?"

A nudge that hopes, "Wouldn't it be great if...?"

To unleash the creativity latent in our profession, we must make room for change. We must stop pushing and pressuring and start setting conditions that foster new ideas and problem-solving.

It requires trust. It requires taking things off of people's plates. It requires leaders who support risks and celebrate ideas. But it's worth it.

Plan for creativity.

> **To unleash the creativity latent in our profession, we must make room for change. We must stop pushing and pressuring and start setting conditions that foster new ideas and problem-solving. #FutureDriven**

CHAPTER 7

Full Responsibility

I believe we have serious ownership challenges in education, both with educators working in schools and with the students we serve. For educators, so much has been pushed down through mandates, accountability systems, and multitudes of negative outside voices that it is easy to lose the passion and purpose that made you become an educator in the first place. I truly believe the people working in schools want to be awesome for kids. They want to crush mediocrity and strive for excellence. Many do just that. But collectively, we need to raise the profession and make our schools shine brighter.

For students, ownership will come through effective leadership in schools. When the adults in the school are working together to model ownership and high expectations, then students will take on more responsibility for learning. Educators need to be fully invested to get students to be fully invested. We've all been guilty of shifting the blame when things aren't working. If it's not working, we need to take collective responsibility. And we need to commit to correct the problem through collective leadership.

We've had multiple teams in our school win district and state championships. Other groups have won or placed at the state and national level in choir, band, debate, culinary, FBLA, FCCLA, FFA and more. When these teams perform at such a high level, you can always count on a high level of ownership from the coaches and the student competitors. You don't perform at a high level by making excuses and passing the buck.

But I have to wonder: how often is the collective commitment in our classrooms on par with the collective commitment elicited from these extracurricular activities? If the level of collective commitment in our classrooms was made visible, would we be championship material? I realize the nature of classroom learning is different than competitive school events that students choose to do. But why not try to bring more of the ownership and high expectations to the classroom that we see in sports, fine arts, debate, etc.?

The pursuit of excellence requires extraordinary ownership. It starts with me as the principal in my building. If something isn't best for our kids and best for learning, I need to own that and take action to make sure we overcome the challenge. I must step up my leadership. And every person who works in the school must do the same. We must believe that nothing is impossible and nothing too difficult if we all pull together.

At the same time, we need to utilize every strategy possible to achieve full ownership from students. There are many ways we can inspire them to be more invested in the process of their own education. To prepare students to be responsible, productive citizens in the future, we must give them opportunities to lead and make decisions now. We must make them partners in the learning process.

Make Us Better

Collective ownership is the most powerful kind. When we are interdependent, we count on each other, believe in each other, lift each other up, that's when we create a dynamic learning environment that can't be stopped. Together we can solve just about any problem and create opportunities far beyond what's common.

My message to our students this year is: *make us better.* You are here to help make this school a better place. You are here to make a difference now. Let's work together. Let's share ideas. Let's make the learning experience better for everyone. I want to hear what you think. I want to know how we can improve. We can do amazing things when we all pull together.

We are going to challenge you, push you, stretch you and cause you to think. We are going to do everything possible to make you better. It's not always going to be comfortable. It's not always going to be easy. We are here to make everyone better. We are all committing to be better. You can help make us better. If we are going to create a future driven school, it's going to take contributions from everyone.

And when our students are *making us better*, they will get better too. The investment in ownership is a game changer. If all the ideas belong to the adults, no wonder kids feel like school is being *done to them*. No wonder they aren't inspired. When students are invested, they will go places we never imagined. We are sending a powerful message: we can't wait to see what you're going to do!

Put Students in the Driver's Seat

If our goal is to create independent, lifelong learners, it's important to create classrooms where students are taking greater ownership of their learning. We know that a student-centered classroom is more effective than a teacher-centered classroom. So how can you put your students in the driver's seat?

Our school went 1:1 with Chromebooks for every student. Some probably assumed this was about keeping up with technology. But the greatest benefit to every student having a device is student agency, the ability for each student to make more of the decisions about the direction of their learning. Access to a device and consequently access to the sum of human knowledge via the internet creates opportunities for empowerment.

But we can't keep teaching the same way and expect empowerment to increase. Just giving a student a device will not lead to more ownership. If nothing changes except we replace textbooks with devices, we have not empowered learning. We have to give up some of our control and help guide and facilitate learning instead of making every decision ourselves.

Here are some questions for you to consider about agency and empowerment in your classroom.

1. How often do students have input on HOW they will learn?
2. How often do students have input on WHAT they will learn?

3. Are students given opportunities to lead conversations?

4. Are classroom goals developed by the teacher alone or in partnership with students?

5. Do students have some time to pursue their own goals?

6. How often do you ask students for feedback on their experience in your classroom?

In classrooms where student ownership has flourished, I've noticed that it's usually because teachers really listen and spend considerable time understanding their students' perspectives, what's important to them, what their experiences with learning have been in the past. There is a feeling that the students and the teacher are co-creating the classroom together, instead of the teacher delivering lessons. What if they teacher had this approach? We can do it any way you want as long as you learn. How would that shift in mindset impact learning?

All teachers I've met want students to take greater ownership. In fact, a common frustration and complaint is that students won't take ownership. They aren't responsible. They won't own their learning. They won't do their homework. They won't participate. They won't engage.

But are we really looking for ownership or simply compliance? We can't expect our students to take greater ownership of learning if we're not willing to empower them as learners. If we want more ownership, it's going to require sharing responsibility and giving up some control.

> ## We can't expect our students to take greater ownership of learning if we're not willing to empower them as learners.
> ## #FutureDriven

This past year every teacher in our building gave a survey to each of their classes to get a sense of how students were experiencing learning in that particular classroom. When students are able to provide input and see that their input is valued and acted upon, they are going to have more ownership of learning. We don't want the school experience to feel like it's being done to students; we want students to feel like they are partners in learning.

To truly empower students means they will have more freedom and choice than they—and you—have been used to. It will require some trial and error to get the results you want. You will have to communicate your vision for learning and regularly revisit why this type of learning is important. Students will want to be spoon-fed information to memorize and regurgitate on tests because this is what they expect from the school experience. But when you make the shift to greater student ownership, it will be extremely rewarding for you and for students. They will feel like they are doing work that matters to them and that makes a difference beyond taking a test or getting a grade.

Avoid the Trash Can Finish

Where does most student work ultimately end up? Unfortunately, most of it is destined for the trash can. It will never be shared with anyone beyond the classroom. The teacher will review it and assess it, and finally, it comes to rest in a landfill. Sometimes, the work will be shared with other students in the classroom. But why aren't we seeking more authentic audiences for student work?

When students know their work will be shared with a real audience, it changes the mindset. Instead of just producing work that is good enough to get the grade, they will want to produce work that represents their best efforts. The sense of audience is an opportunity to practice empathy, to picture the project through the end user's eyes. It's what professionals do in their work all the time. Our students need to be practicing the skills that all people use when they are completing a project or developing a product that will no doubt be presented to a real audience.

> *If students are sharing their work with the world, they want it to be good. If they are just sharing it with you, they want it to be good enough. —Rushton Hurley*

And there are more ways than ever to share student work. With social media and other digital platforms, student work can be shared across the world. Students can create blogs, produce podcasts, or compile digital portfolios.

Twitter is a great way to share out links or images of student work. The #Comments4Kids hashtag is one great way to connect with audiences and get feedback too.

I read that in the future your online presence will replace the traditional resume. Employers will just look for what you've accomplished online. What evidence is there of your skills? But most students (and most teachers) haven't done anything intentional to establish a digital presence or personal brand. Your classroom could help change that. You can find ways to share student work so that their great ideas and best efforts can be accessed in the present and the future.

Besides digital sharing of work, there are other ways to make learning visible and include real audiences. Elementary schools are great at displaying student work throughout the school. Why don't more secondary schools do this? One idea a teacher developed in our school invites professionals in our community to examine student projects. It's kind of like the TV show *Shark Tank*, with students pitching their ideas to a panel of "sharks." Schools can also have makerfaires or other showcase events where student work is on display for parents and community.

Avoiding the trash-can-finish might be as simple as a Tweet or as complex as a school maker faire. Everything students do can't be shared out, but we need to start sharing more. It brings relevance to learning and allows kids to contribute ideas and products to the world right now. Students shouldn't have to wait until they are out of school to make valuable contributions.

Whoever Is Doing the Talking is Doing the Learning[1]

Our kids were talking as the food was passed. Ray (step-dad/granddad) was working his way through a joke he was telling. When I commented on the distracted kids, Ray chuckled reassuringly, "That's okay. The only place where one person talks at a time is a classroom."

I was momentarily stunned. I immediately thought of the professional relevance of the words. Ray's comment was totally in jest. But there is a sad element of truth to this, at least in many traditional classrooms. I could see that this statement was profound in a sense.

As you might expect, often the one person who is doing most of the talking is the teacher.

Students sit in desks, with materials out in front. They are slouched over, eyes tired but gazing toward the front of the room. That is where the teacher remains.

Even when students are invited to speak, it's a response to the teacher. Maybe a couple of words. Answering a question. Nothing that resembles an authentic conversation.

On task? Yes, you could say so. Engaged. Not in the least.

It's true that the one doing most of the talking is also doing most of the learning. Students have a lot to say, and the skilled teacher creates conditions for students to process what they are learning through conversations.

In the classroom of a distinguished teacher, "Students assume considerable responsibility for the success of the discussion, initiating topics, and making unsolicited contributions."[2]

Teacher Knows Best

I had a conversation not too long ago with an educator who pushed back a little on the topic of student empowerment. The teacher asserted that he went to school to be trained as a professional, is an expert in his discipline, and knows the best methods and strategies for teaching the students in his classes. The line of thinking seemed to indicate that students are not equipped to take a more active role in directing their own learning.

In another conversation with a different educator, I suggested that students and teachers should partner in the learning process and that students' voices should be heard. But there was some push back. The person shared that some teachers would not like the term partner with students. It seems too much like students and teachers are on the same level.

Of course, I realize teachers assume a position of authority inherent in their role. And while teachers should seek to share power with students, they should also maintain a leadership role. When necessary, they can direct, guide, or even say no. But when teachers truly honor student voices and really listen, it's often amazing to see the initiative, wisdom, and commitment students will display.

I guess you can see I'm a big believer in student empowerment. Actually, I'm a believer in student and teacher empowerment, and empowerment in general.

I believe empowerment is one of the essential purposes of pursuing education. The more you know, the better you are equipped to make good decisions, by your own choice.

Empowerment is increasing the ability to act on one's own behalf or on the behalf of the community to accomplish a goal or create an outcome. It is an essential part of our freedom and liberty in this country. In fact, it is wrong to keep capable people controlled or limited when they can do it on their own.

When students are empowered learners, we equip them to make positive choices, to take control of their circumstances, and to go forward with their learning and goals. It's empowering!

Any Way You Want

In the future, no one is going to care how our students learned what they know. No one is going to care if they learned the skills in a classroom, online, or from some other source. People will want to know what you can do. What skills do you have? What can you bring to our project? Why would we want you on our team? They will look at your work, your portfolio, your online presence to assess your capabilities. It won't be about the degree or the credential as much as it will be about what value you bring.

What if teachers designed learning with that in mind? What if we allow students to learn however it works best for them as long as they are learning? There would still need to be accountability, but not for how you learn it, but that you show you've learned it. I think this is the type of learning we will see more in the future. Students will make meaning of their learning and share what they know in a variety of ways.

---

9 Reasons Educators Should Empower Students

1. To develop more independent learners.

The best learning is not dependent learning. It is learning that is self-directed and intrinsically motivated. School should be a place where students are expected to take greater ownership of learning.

2. To create lifelong learners.

As I reflect on my school days, very little I experienced led me to be the life-long learner I am today. That's not to say I didn't learn quite a bit in school, but I didn't learn how to pursue learning for life. I learned that outside of school. It doesn't have to be that way.

3. To help students learn to make good decisions.

Students need practice making decisions about their own learning. They need to learn about their own strengths and weakness and how their decisions affect self and others. When there are few choices in learning, students are being robbed of the opportunity to grow as a decision-maker.

4. To foster more relevance in learning.

When students are empowered, learning becomes more relevant. Instead of just doing something as I'm told, I am able to learn things that are of interest and value to me. Teachers can help provide the context to expand and challenge the interests of students but not to make all the decisions for them. I believe students would take a harder look at what is really valuable if they were given more opportunities to be empowered.

5. To help students find their passions.

I believe this is one of the most important parts of a well-rounded education. Students need to find things they are passionate about. Learning is lifeless for the most part unless there is passion. When students discover passions, they will care more and do more. If I'm passionate about something, I will invest in that passion even when it's hard. Students will be more likely to find passions when they are empowered as learners.

6. To learn resilience.

Resilience develops from suffering a failure but caring enough to press on in the face of difficulty. School that is mostly compliance-driven results in students who want to do just enough to get by, or they want to take shortcuts or work the system to get a certain result (a good grade or a diploma for instance). Learning that is empowered results in students who will strive to overcome obstacles and do more than is expected. Resilience is closely tied to sense of purpose, support from others, and a positive outlook.

7. To develop empathy.

I believe empowered learners are more likely to understand and exhibit empathy. Empowered learners see how they can make a difference in the world. They grasp how their learning can impact others. How it can help a friend, or solve a problem, or challenge someone's thinking. If we want to create students who are world-changers we must give them opportunities to make a difference right now. Students need to have opportunities, as part of their education, to recognize injustice and then do something about it.

8. To promote leadership.

When I talk with students about leadership, I can see that many view it as having and wielding power. I think much of this thinking comes from the experience they've had in school where most all of the power is consolidated with teachers and administration. When we empower learners, we share power with them to help them develop the skills to own power and also share it with others. It's not about telling someone else what to do. It's about working with others to accomplish a greater good. At its best, it starts with humility and service. Students need to see this modeled, and they need to have the opportunity to practice it as well.

9. To develop better global citizens.

Young people want to make a difference in the world, but they are immobilized by a system that tells them every move to make. Empowerment allows students to make a difference now. Empowerment asks students, "What problem will you solve? How can you make the world a better place?" But there is a choice. Students will learn to be better citizens when they have the chance to lead and speak up on causes that are important to them.

10. To practice creativity.

Creativity requires unconventional thinking and will not thrive in a compliance-based culture. Empowerment promotes creative thinking. It's not about finding right answers. It's about looking at problems in novel ways.

11. To cultivate curiosity.

Curiosity is also supported through decisions that empower others. We aren't likely to be curious about things that aren't personally meaningful. But when we are empowered to pursue our own questions, to investigate, to explore ideas, then our curiosity becomes an incredible pathway to learning.

What Do You Think?

For the past couple of years, we have been growing a computer science program at Bolivar High School. We are very excited about the opportunities this provides for our students. Computer science skills are in high demand. And there are computer-science related career opportunities in just about every industry. But learning to code can be challenging. It requires problem-solving and perseverance.

When students get stuck on something, they will often ask their teacher what to do. And her response is to ask them a question: What do you think?

She wants them to learn to solve problems without expecting the teacher to immediately swoop in and rescue them at the first difficulty.

Don't rob your students of the struggle. They need to grow stronger at persevering and solving problems. Students have greater ownership when they press on in the face of a setback or problem. Students will rise to your expectations. Don't let them take the easy way out. Make them think.

Let them try it on their own. Develop the mindset that they are learners. I've heard students comment, he or she didn't teach me. They normally say this when the teacher has asked them to figure it out.

Are You Strengths-Based or Deficit-Driven?

An important part of being an excellent teacher is attempting to create conditions that cause all kids to want to learn more. If we consistently develop each student's desire to know, they will eventually become unstoppable learners. We can never assume the motivation and engagement of students is a fixed characteristic.

Never assume some students are just naturally curious and others are not. Instead, always be striving to unleash the natural curiosity and wonder in every learner.

One reason some students withhold effort and engagement is a feeling that they will not be successful as a learner. When students don't believe in their own ability to learn, they tend to avoid learning. School has a way of sorting students into smart/not-smart, learners/non-learners, capable/not-capable. At least, that's how many students feel.

Unfortunately, for too many students, school has felt like a place where they are constantly reminded of what they aren't good at. And that needs to change if we hope to create learning environments where all students become curious, enthusiastic, and engaged learners.

What if every educator in your school committed to make learning a strengths-based endeavor? What kind of place would your school be? Talk with your team about the belief statements I share below. How can these translate into a different approach to learning for your school?

1. Every student has unique gifts and talents as a learner.
2. Students who are confident learners will learn more. They will want to learn more.

3. Each student needs to feel like he/she can be successful.

4. Educators should recognize different aptitudes and adjust accordingly. One-size-fits-all doesn't work.

5. Learning is built on strengths and not deficits. Are you reminding students more of their assets or their liabilities?

6. We should focus on what a child can do, instead of what he/she cannot do.

7. Teachers should design learning experiences that allow students to use strengths to make meaning. Allow students to enter the problem in a way that is familiar and go from there.

8. It's impossible to develop an effective learning experience if we treat a classroom full of students like they all have the same strengths.

9. Success breeds success. So if students have success with a task in their strength area, they are more likely to take on a task that isn't in their strength area.

10. We all give and withhold effort depending on our own feelings of talent, skill, and efficacy.

11. Seek to understand how students learn best, and help students understand how they learn best.

Excellence In Action

It's impossible to achieve excellence in your school without developing student ownership. You might have great test scores, pass your state's accountability system, and have a polite, friendly climate. But you won't have excellence. Excellence doesn't come by compliance. It doesn't come from following instructions or using a formula to succeed.

True excellence is personal.

It's your best, not someone else's idea of your best.

Excellence isn't working hard to do what you're told.

Excellence is working hard at something that's important to you.

Excellence isn't getting a high score or a good grade.

Excellence is doing work that matters to you.

Excellence isn't winning or being better than someone else.

Excellence is being the best version of you.

Excellence isn't being something that you're not.

Excellence is a calling.

When you strive for excellence, success will follow. And when you have a school culture where excellence is the norm, your school will be a place of excellence.

Best Work

Most everyone likes to work with the best students. We all know there are some students who are easier to teach. They come ready to learn. They are motivated. They want to do good work. They want to learn more. I remember my very first year teaching who my best student was. He was a seventh grader who literally knew more about world history than I did. But he wasn't arrogant or difficult to teach. He wanted to learn from me. But honestly, he was going to learn no matter what I did.

I also remember the most challenging student I had my first year. He wasn't really interested in learning. He didn't have much parent support. He was in trouble all the time. He was very mouthy. For the most part, I liked him. But I also wasn't sure how to handle him. It was my first year. He didn't respond well to me when I became "large and in charge." That's how I thought I'd make him mind. And as a result, I wrote him up to the office on a semi-regular basis.

I'd like to think I could do much better with that difficult student today. I remember how frustrated he made me. I think I resented how he made me feel. I felt disrespected. I felt like he was trying to destroy my classroom. And he probably was. But it probably had more to do with the needs not being met in his life than anything to do with me or my class.

A student's behavior usually says far more about what they are going through than what they are trying to put you through.

Instead of viewing our most challenging students as a burden, what if we viewed them as an opportunity to do our best work?

What if we viewed the tough ones as an opportunity to make an even bigger difference? Who needs us most? The top students are going to succeed and do well, almost in spite of us. We aren't going to slow them down. But the students who are struggling and hurting and don't have anyone in their corner, they need us the most. Of course, we want to help all students succeed. But let's remember the toughest students provide an opportunity for us to make the biggest difference.

Change Agents

You will never raise student performance by lowering expectations. Extraordinary ownership means high expectations for all. But it starts with accepting full responsibility for oneself.

Time capsule teachers actually have high expectations. But their high expectations are mostly focused outward. They expect everyone else to change to meet their view of the world. If something outside of them were different, a problem could be solved. They expect students to change, parents to change, administrators to change, everyone to change, except the person in the mirror. They want their comfort protected and preserved.

Likewise, time machine teachers have high expectations. But their high expectations are focused on what they can do. They are willing to move. They see themselves as change agents. They take full responsibility for the things they can control. They realize they have the power, by their own thoughts and actions, to create change. A common narrative in time travel stories is for a protagonist to visit the past to have some impact on how history unfolds. Of course, time machine teachers can't literally travel to the past, but they do realize how their actions now will impact how a child's story will play out in the future.

If we want to see students rise to greater challenges, we must be willing to accept greater challenges. If we want students to take full ownership, educators need to take full ownership. We are the architects of our lives. It's easy to see how everyone else needs to change. But we are not victims. We have far more power than we ever realize. Far more than our circumstances, it is our thoughts, our choices, and our attitudes that determine our destiny and the destinies of our students.

CHAPTER 8

Adaptable Learners

My dad grew up on the farm working from dawn till dusk, going to school, showing cattle, and driving tractors. My dad really struggled in school. I often wondered if he would've been diagnosed with some type of learning disability if he were in school today, maybe ADHD or dyslexia. He couldn't spell, struggled to pronounce certain words, and had many behaviors consistent with attention disorders.

But he was a standout at connecting with people. And he was successful as a farm kid. His cattle consistently won blue ribbons. He was especially proud of his tractor driving championship at the county fair. His dream was to have his own farm and be an auctioneer. And he had all the skills he needed to be incredibly successful at that.

But when he was 18 years old, he had a serious accident and flipped his car. His faith was very important to him, and for some time he had felt a nudge that he was supposed to go into Christian ministry. But he didn't want to give up his other dreams. And he didn't feel he was equipped to be a pastor. That would probably mean going to college. School was not his thing.

But after the car accident, he was more open to the idea. He felt like God was getting his attention. He was ordained as a minister later that year and left for college soon after.

It took my dad nearly 8 years to get through college. It was a struggle. He was pastoring small country churches at the same time, so he had a lot of responsibility. After he finished his undergraduate degree, he went on to seminary in Louisville. And he finished a degree there, also.

Even though he struggled in school and didn't have the strongest academic skills, he never gave up. He had the ability to persevere. He worked very hard to overcome the obstacles that were in his way because it mattered to him. He didn't have to finish college, but he felt it was important.

He was able to adapt to his own struggles and to the challenges of his circumstances. And equally important, he built on the strengths he had to great effectiveness. He could talk to anyone. He cared deeply about people. And he made everyone feel important, no matter their station in life. He was equally at ease with the doctor or the dog catcher.

Acceleration

Since we live in an age of innovation, a practical education must prepare a person for work that does not yet exist and cannot yet be clearly defined. —Peter Drucker

The world is changing faster than ever before. Prior to the industrial revolution, changes occurred so slowly they were barely noticeable. But they were still faster than in more distant times. As new technology emerges, the rate of change only accelerates. The possibilities of what's next are built on what currently is. Technology builds on the previous technology.

Thomas Friedman illustrates this in his book *Thank You for Being Late*. He contrasts the typewriter and the iPhone. Most students today have probably never used a typewriter. It is no longer a relevant technology in a world of computers and printers. The typewriter emerged over a period of decades in the late 1800's with several inventors contributing to a commercially successful tool. In over 100 years of relevance, the typewriter changed very little. The basic conventions remained the same.

Compare that with the emergence of the iPhone, which was released in 2007. It was a device that had earth-shattering implications. It began the age of truly mobile computing. There are billions of people using a smartphone on a daily basis and the number continues to swell even in the least developed countries. In a decade, the iPhone has undergone numerous iterations. While the basic concept of the device remains the same, its utility is immensely changed. A first generation iPhone went from being a game-changer to obsolete in a very short time. On to the next generation. On to better, faster, more powerful.

Essential Skills

Test scores tell us little about our children's readiness for a complex, uncertain world. Test scores reveal who is good at taking tests, and that doesn't always transfer to authentic situations beyond school. So what is the best predictor of future success? What skills would we see in a student and know they are going to be successful? What would we look for? What would make them ready for anything they might face?

Although the technical skills might open doors for our students, it's the people skills that will determine just how far they will go. Some have referred to these skills as soft skills. I think they are success skills or essential skills. Calling them soft skills makes them sound like they are fluffy, dreamy, and sentimental. Not to be taken seriously. These non-cognitive factors are never measured on standardized tests, but that doesn't mean they shouldn't be important to educators. If we are concerned with preparing students for life beyond school, these skills are critical.

I had the opportunity to join with other educators in our area for an industry tour. We visited companies in healthcare, manufacturing, technology, and more. Every employer expressed concerns about the soft skills gap. We can train the technical skills, they said. But we want to hire people who are dependable, self-motivated, team oriented, flexible, organized, and who can use feedback to improve.

Best-selling author and psychologist Daniel Goleman has written extensively about the need for these personal skills, skills like empathy and emotional intelligence:

> If your emotional abilities aren't in hand, if you don't have self-awareness, if you are not able to manage your distressing emotions, if you can't have empathy and have effective relationships, then no matter how smart you are, you're not going to get very far.

Goleman's research has shown that emotional intelligence is twice as important as cognitive factors in predicting outstanding employee performance.[1]

If you work with someone who lacks these skills, you know how important they are. If you encounter someone in your day who doesn't have their emotional abilities in hand, you know how disruptive that can be. It is critical for students to have opportunities to learn these skills and practice them in school. We help students improve personal mastery as we teach academic skills. It's not one or the other. It's both. But how do we do that? I am suggesting a three step process. Teach. Model. Reflect.

Teach

Instead of just getting frustrated when students don't have the personal skills we would like, we need to be intentional about teaching these skills. Some of that can be done in a systematic way like a character trait of the month that is the subject of lessons or discussions. But I think it's even better when we use those teachable moments, when we embed learning about these skills. Tie in the essential skills with events in your classroom, school, community, or with events in the larger world. But talk about these factors all the time. Always remember you are teaching kids first, then curriculum. Don't place your curricular goals ahead of the moment when you could teach a life changing lesson.

Stories are powerful for learning these lessons. Tell your own stories of perseverance. Look to the lives of famous people and how they overcame obstacles, helped others, and continued to learn and grow. Have students read about personal mastery and self-improvement. Students need more opportunities to think about how to learn and how to develop themselves to reach their potential.

Model

Your example is your greatest influence. What you say is important, but what you do speaks even louder. When you show your students how you are committed to growing, it is a powerful example. When you admit your mistakes, it shows growth is more important than being perfect. When you accept feedback well and use it to get better, it encourages students to do the same.

We can't expect students to improve their personal skills if we aren't willing to do the same. None of us is perfect. No one shows up every day without some rough edges, some areas to improve, some opportunities for growth. Make your own growth visible to students and see what impact that has on their learning and the culture of your classroom. Be willing to learn right alongside your students.

Reflect

Effective people are reflective people. As John Dewey observed, "We don't learn from experience, we learn from reflecting on experience." It's so important to continually reflect on cause and effect relationships. Our students need to see the connection between their actions and their outcomes. Many seem to believe that things just happen by chance. They have a fixed mindset. They don't see the connection between what they do and how things turn out.

Have students write about their successes and failures. Have them talk about what worked well and what didn't. Make them think. Help them process the connections between what successful people do and how successful people think.

Reflection is one of the most neglected areas in education. We are always going forward to the next lesson, the next standard, the next assignment. But we must make time to reflect and help our students reflect on how they can be more effective, successful people.

Learn, Unlearn, Relearn

Prior to 1940, most Americans did not attend school past the 8th grade. High school attainment rates rose steadily in the years of the Cold War. But even then, school was for 12 years or maybe on to college, but the need to constantly learn and adapt was not a consideration. You basically learned everything you needed while you were in school. You trained for your job or profession and then went to work and remained in the same job doing the same type of work for many years.

In our current age of acceleration, the need to continue to learn is essential. People are upset when jobs disappear and understandably so. When you invest in skills and training, you want to be able to count on employment. But there are no guarantees when the shifts are happening across industries and markets. Sometimes the jobs go overseas where they can be done cheaper. But often, the industry completely changes. The work is different. Or, it's not needed at all. Or, a machine is now capable of doing the work once done entirely by people.

Many jobs as we know them are changing dramatically. Automation has already transformed the auto industry. It takes as little at 15 man hours for some automobile plants to produce a car. Robots are positioned to replace or augment trades like masonry and house painting. Drones are expected to deliver packages. And up to 20 million self-driving cars may be on the road in less than a decade. Automated technology is transforming the world as we know it.

The world is quickly changing and the world of work is changing with it. There is no need to work in an office 9-5 when you can work anytime and anyplace. Opportunities to climb the corporate ladder may be fewer, while opportunities to create your own ladder increase. While we face many challenges, there will also many opportunities. But the only way to take advantage of what's possible is to always remain a learner. The ability to remain relevant as a worker will be dependent on being relevant as a learner. Lifelong learning will be essential for employment.

Adaptable Curriculum

I recently reviewed another school's curriculum for high school English, as part of an effort to make our curriculum better. It was supposed to be an outstanding curriculum. The school has a great reputation and high achievement. After I spent some time examining it, I couldn't help but think, how different is this than the curriculum that I had in high school English class many years ago?

What about blogging? Social media? Digital literacy? Publishing online? Ebooks? How much of the traditional English curriculum is only relevant if the student's goal is to be an English professor? Some of it is relevant. Some of it isn't. A similar critique could be done for other curriculum areas. Are we developing curriculum that is relevant to today and looking to tomorrow?

If we want adaptable learners, our curriculum needs to adapt. It shouldn't be the same curriculum we taught 10 years ago. Some skills are timeless, but how they are applied and the ways they are used keep changing. We need to create learning experiences that reflect the types of platforms, processes, and possibilities that professionals are actually using today. Our classrooms shouldn't be like time capsules. They shouldn't preserve a curriculum meant for another time.

Instead, our curriculum should help students learn to adapt and create new possibilities. It should be like a time machine. It should take students to new places. It should embrace imagination and creativity. You won't get ahead or stay ahead in today's world if you hold on tightly to what you already know. The pace of change will require rapid learning. It will require you to be future driven.

How do we decide what to teach students? Things are changing so fast, the information they need today may not even be relevant tomorrow. But they will always need to think critically. They will always need to communicate ideas. They will need to show empathy and accept people who are different.

We live in an age of information abundance. We can easily access information at any time. At the tip of our fingers, we have access to unlimited information. With just a few keystrokes we can search for whatever we need to know. But understanding is more elusive. Understanding requires deeper knowing. It requires us to make meaning. The curriculum should seek to help students make meaning about the world around them.

Let's think about assessments. If students use their phones on a test, we call that cheating. If they get help from someone else, we call that cheating. In the world outside school, that's common practice. That's expected. It's leveraging resources. It's a valuable skill.

Professionals are never told to only use only what's in their head. They are expected to use all available resources to solve problems and develop the best possible solutions. If students can do well on your test just by having access to Google, maybe your test needs to change. If the goal is to develop transferable skills, create assessments that require students to apply what they know. If you must give tests, make them like almost nothing you've practiced. Have them draw on the skills you've practiced but force them to transfer to a new context.

Riding a Bike

It's much easier to adapt to change when you're moving. If you're in time machine mode, you're going to be able to achieve what Eric "Astro" Teller, CEO of Google's X research and development lab, refers to as dynamic stability. You're moving, you're going places. Thomas Friedman relates Teller's ideas on adapting in his book *Thank You For Being Late*.[2] The accelerating speed of science and technology innovations is outpacing the capacity of most of us to adjust to the changes.

But it's even tougher if you're a time capsule. If you're stuck, you can't adapt at all. Teller describes how we need dynamic stability, like when we ride a bike. It's really tough to balance a bicycle when it's not moving. But when you get going, it's much easier. You are actually more stable when you are moving than when you are standing still. We are in an era of persistent destabilization, and our kids will need to be better able to cope with this reality. With dynamic stability, it won't seem so unusual to constantly adjust to change. They will just keep moving.

It's time to act, or you will be acted upon. Change is not optional. Sometimes when I'm talking about how we need to change, it draws a sharp reply,

"Well, we don't need change just for the sake of change." In a sense, I agree with this. Random change isn't usually helpful. But I think that type of phrase is often a deliberate resistance to any change.

Google didn't have to pour millions into new product development. They had the dominant market position on internet search. They could've just watched the money pile up. But they realized that things are dynamic. What's next can make even a Google obsolete if they don't continue evolving and adjusting. Education has been as static as just about any industry. Time capsule thinking keeps us frozen. We would do well to try dynamic stability and see what happens. We've been trying to get better at many of the same things for years. Maybe it's time to try some completely different things.

Failure to Adapt

People who aren't willing to adapt will miss so many opportunities and possibilities. The technology of the last 10 years has provided unbelievable opportunities for me. But that would never have happened if I kept doing the same things I was doing in the 10 years prior to that. I tried different things. I was looking for ways to leverage my skills using technology. At one point, I thought online classes were unlikely to ever really catch on. But now I've taught hundreds of graduate students online. It's amazing that I teach for a university hundreds of miles away from my home. And I learned about the opportunity because of a Twitter post that mentioned the job was available.

Social media has allowed me to connect with other educators far beyond what I ever imagined. There have been many benefits that have come to me and my school because of our engagement with the available tools. These opportunities only happen because we are willing to learn and try new things.

Even this book is an example of taking advantage of the opportunities that are available. In the past, it would be impossible to publish to a broad audience without the help of a traditional publisher. But today that is possible. In fact, many bestselling books have been self-published.

But with emerging technologies and opportunities, you can't wait for someone to give you instructions on what to do. You have to jump in and be a learner. Our students need to learn this type of initiative. What do you do when there aren't specific instructions for what to do? We must overcome the fear of change and the desire to hold on to the way things are. We have to be okay with some discomfort and with making some mistakes. I've had some experiences that didn't work out. I've made some mistakes; that's for sure. But it wasn't because I wasn't trying.

When we are flexible, versatile, and adaptable, we will create value. We will be able to enter new arenas and take on new challenges and handle changes in our career and personal life. Your ability to adapt is one of the most important ways you show that you are a learner. Your ability to adapt will take you places, you'll make a bigger difference, and you'll help others in ways you never thought possible.

Nonconformity

Experts are often wrong. Conventional thinking isn't always correct. Challenge assumptions and norms. Challenge your own thinking. Invite others to challenge your perspective. The only way to better decisions is through better thinking. And we need to get all the ideas on the table. There are too many examples of how the experts got it wrong. I'd rather be considered a learner than an expert.

As Henry Ford recounted, when the idea of the automobile was being formulated, what people thought they wanted was faster horses. A prominent bank president reportedly said the automobile was a novelty and that the horse was here to stay as the best means of transportation. It's so easy to get comfortable with how we see the world.

School has been a place where conformity has been reinforced. Control and compliance were valued over original ideas or divergent thinking. Teachers were the expert in the room. They distributed knowledge to students. And this fit with the industrial age. Schools were factories, not think tanks. Students had to rely on teachers to inform them.

But the world has changed and so should classrooms. Teachers will still hold great value, but it won't be as the sole purveyors of knowledge. It will be to help students learn to use available resources, to find their strengths, and to cause deeper thinking. We need to celebrate originality and allow students to pursue learning in ways that are personal and meaningful.

Bury Can't

We are living in an unbelievable age of opportunity and possibility. We never want our students to place limits on themselves and what they are capable of accomplishing. And we certainly don't want to be the ones placing the limits on them. We need to remind them every chance we get they can do amazing things. We need to encourage them to find their gifts and use them to reach higher. We need to crush the limits and help them believe in themselves.

Years ago, when I was the principal of middle school students, we were concerned about the mindset of our students. It was years before I knew about Carol Dweck or a Growth Mindset. But we all knew that our students were reluctant to take risks. They didn't believe in their own abilities. They weren't persisting through problems. It seemed like the response to any challenge was "I can't." Those words were completely unacceptable to me.

So we took a risk of our own. I had someone make a small cardboard coffin (yes a coffin!!!), and on the outside, it said *R.I.P Can't*. We planned a time to have our memorial service where we said goodbye to *Can't* forever. All the 7th and 8th graders were part of this ceremony. I don't remember exactly how I eulogized our dearly departed word. But it probably went something like this.

> *It's difficult to describe how Can't has impacted all our lives. He has always been there for us, clinging to us, especially in the hard times. He became one of our favorite words. I'm sure we all relied on him too often. What will we do without him? Well, the possibilities are endless. We can do just about anything we can imagine. That's how he would want it. So today we say farewell, and we will never speak of Can't again.*

And then we literally buried *Can't* right behind the school in his tiny little coffin. Of course, the students loved the whole thing. They thought it was about the funniest thing ever. Especially when I had some teachers lay flowers on the coffin and wipe away pretend tears. You get the idea. It was over the top. But I hope it made a strong impression on the students. I hope it caused them to think about their attitudes and their potential.

For students to thrive in an unpredictable world, they must be adaptable learners. They must adjust to the changes that are happening and be lifelong learners. And an important part of that mindset is their belief in their own ability to learn. They will never reach their potential if they embrace can't. Instead, they must believe they can. We must show them they can. Our most urgent task is to make sure our students know how to learn.

For students to thrive in an unpredictable world, they must be adaptable learners. #FutureDriven

CHAPTER 9

Everyone as a Learner

Every future-driven educator must focus on learning, not just learning for their students, but also for themselves. My first year as a teacher was in a 7th-grade social studies classroom.

The previous teacher, Mr. Page, was a beloved educator. More precisely, he was a legend. He had taught for many years and immediately people would smile at the mention of his name. They would begin to tell stories they remembered from his classroom. The one story they would all recount was how he had created a miniature model of a guillotine and when introducing the French Revolution he would demonstrate the apparatus with a Barbie doll filled with ketchup. Off with her head! You can imagine how much 7th graders loved that.

Anytime I would meet someone new in the community, of course, I would share that I was a new teacher. When they found out I was replacing Mr. Page, they would immediately respond, "You've got big shoes to fill." I heard that over and over leading up to my first year in teaching.

Those first years were tough. I remember feeling inadequate, worn out, discouraged, and alone in my teaching assignment. I felt like I should know how to handle everything in the classroom. But my classes were handing it to me. I never thought I would have discipline issues, but I was writing office referrals on a regular basis.

I share my struggles to illustrate that a willingness to grow is really the most important thing you need to be successful as an educator. It didn't happen for me right away, but I did improve in my first few years. I've continued to grow and when I look back 5, or 10, or 15 years, I see how my thinking has changed and how my skills have improved. In that first year, I thought I needed to have it all together.

Past, Present, Future

Learn from the past. But don't get stuck there. Don't be locked in a time-capsule. You will never reach your potential or help others reach their potential if you are living in the past. When we hold onto the past too tightly, we either romanticize it or demonize it. Either we put the past on a pedestal or we relive the pain of the past over and over. With either approach, we are stuck, and we aren't keeping the past in proper perspective. The past should be seen for both its good and its bad. We should count our blessings for the good and strive to learn from the bad.

Live in the present. Today is the day you must own. Being future driven is actually more about what you do today than what happens tomorrow. If you live fully in the present, you can stop worrying about the future and stop regretting the past and just make the most of each moment. At the end of each day, be satisfied that you have contributed something meaningful to yourself and to others. Work hard. Do your best. Make people your priority. Being future driven is making decisions today that will make you and others stronger in the long run.

Look to the future. I love movies that inspire. As a kid, I remember coming home from seeing *Rocky* and seeing myself as the champ. I was doing sit-ups and pushups while *Eye of the Tiger* played from my boom box. *Hoosiers* is one of my all-time favorite films. It's about second chances, the pride of community, and the underdog achieving the impossible. As a former basketball coach, it was one I could connect with easily. Shawshank Redemption is another film with a powerful message. Nothing could be much worse than being wrongfully sentenced to prison, but Andy Dufresne never loses hope. He has a vision of freedom. And because of his hope and faith that it would happen, it happens.

Each movie is about overcoming odds to reach for dreams. If you can dream it, you can do it. It's natural to have fear or anxiety about the future, or to place limits on ourselves or others and what can be accomplished. But we are really only limited by what we are willing to desire. We have to allow ourselves to dream big and pursue those dreams daily. If we want a better future, we have to envision a better future and believe in a better future. It's a mistake to ever believe you are finished growing. You can unleash your dreams and make an extraordinary impact on the world. Be future-focused and dream big.

> *Leaders are fascinated by the future. You are a leader if and only if, you are restless for change, impatient for progress and deeply dissatisfied with the status quo. Because in your head, you can see a better future. The friction between 'what is' and 'what could be' burns you, stirs you up, propels you. This is leadership.*
> *—Marcus Buckingham*

Great Teachers Are Always Improving

No amount of success is enough for great teachers. They are always looking for ways to improve learning for students. They are always growing. They never believe they have arrived and figured it all out. They never think there is not room to improve.

Great teachers are great learners, too. They don't wait for the school to 'develop' them. We've all been to mind-numbing professional development sessions. We've also observed educators who don't make an effort to engage in professional learning. Maybe you've been professionally disengaged. Maybe the culture of your school doesn't reward growth and progress for teachers.

It makes me sad that so many educators have lost sight of why they became teachers in the first place. You can make a huge impact, and one way you can do that is to continue to learn and grow.

Don't expect your school to own your personal growth. Ultimately, it is your responsibility to be a learner. It's up to you to become your best. Of course, every school should support educator learning, but with all the tools available today, you can connect and learn no matter what your school is doing to support your growth. Take the initiative to be a learner.

Teachers and Students Learning Side-by-Side

A perfect day in a classroom is when both teacher and students are learning together. When there is a culture of inquiry focused on questions and problems, it is only natural that teachers are learning too. They don't have all the answers because no one knows what the answers will be until deep thinking leads to novel solutions.

How great is it when students feel like they get to lead learning? It's very empowering for students to have the opportunity to help the teacher learn something, too. When we started our student tech team, one of the first activities was for the students to lead sessions at our district PD event. The students were so excited to share their knowledge with teachers. They did a session on Google Chrome apps and extensions. I think the students were convinced they had the best session of the day. And teachers were very enthusiastic about what they learned, too. It was a great experience for everyone.

But students and teachers learning together shouldn't be reserved for a special event. It should be something that happens on a routine basis. The teacher doesn't have to be in the role of purveyor of knowledge anymore.

I wonder how often students think about teachers as learners, too. Do they think teachers know everything? Or, that they only learn at conferences? Or in teacher meetings? Shouldn't students see teachers learning every day? Seeing teachers learning alongside students sets a powerful example.

What if We Had Genius Hour for Teachers?

We have time built into our weekly schedule for teacher collaboration, and that's a good thing. But all good things need to be reinvented or at least reinvigorated to make them better. We need to be creative to make the use of time and resources as valuable as possible. Our weekly collaboration time grew out of the Professional Learning Communities movement, and our school has benefited from the PLC structure. But I see a new vision for collaboration and growth emerging.

What if we had Genius Hour for teachers, a time for professionals to work on passion projects? I've seen this idea tossed around on various Twitter chats, and it's reportedly been done in forward-thinking schools. The idea is to empower people to use part of their productive work time to pursue projects they believe are most meaningful for them and for their students.

It could be done independently or collaboratively, with several teachers joining together to share work on a project. The point is that time would be devoted to creativity and innovation and developing ideas and projects that are interesting and personally motivating for teachers.

In the PLC model, teachers are expected to collaboratively plan instruction, write assessments, and analyze data as part of a team. Without question, this team approach was a step in the right direction. Prior to PLC, there was a significant isolation problem in schools. Teachers were jokingly described as a set of independent contractors united by a common parking lot. There seemed to be very little sharing or collaboration in schools.

And yet some of the silos still exist, even though people are sitting in the same room on a semi-regular basis. But overall the idea of working together, sharing ideas, and developing a collective sense of shared ownership has improved because of PLC's.

But the PLC model also seems to reinforce the industrial narrative of schooling with every teacher implementing a "guaranteed and viable" curriculum and "delivering" instruction to students. In this paradigm, all students need to learn the same information in a similar time frame as demonstrated on a common assessment. Those students who don't meet the proper timeline receive intervention to ensure that mastery is attained.

The PLC method seems designed for efficiency and consistency, but not for inspiring creativity or knowledge creation. With Genius Hour, the opportunity for out-of-the-box thinking would be emphasized. Teachers would have time to pursue creative ideas for enhancing student learning above and beyond the measurable outcomes of a benchmark assessment.

Here are five reasons we need to explore Genius Hour for teachers:

1. If we want to encourage creative thinking with students, we need to start with teachers. Learning is not something that can be "delivered." Learning is inspired and based on curiosity and creativity.

2. We need to encourage learning not as a checklist of standards but as a life-long pursuit. Our goal should be learning for life, both for our students and teachers. Too much learning is focused on preparing for a test.

3. Teamwork would be even stronger in schools if teachers were allowed to contribute based on their strengths and not a predefined structure. People love to contribute to a team when they feel their work is valued and there is a shared purpose and interdependence among team members.

4. When we empower teachers to do personally meaningful work, they will more fully reach their professional potential as educators. When there is a personal connection to one's work, on an emotional level, there is a far greater chance that commitment and passion will increase as well.

5. Instead of focusing on results (student achievement data), we need to focus on the process (better learning experiences for students). Whether it's from Daniel Pink's *Drive* or Carol Dweck's *Mindset*, there is compelling evidence that high performance is more likely when we focus on growth, embrace mistakes as an opportunity to learn, and provide a professional culture that embraces autonomy, mastery, and sense of purpose.

Does Your PD Honor Teachers As Learners?

For the past couple of years, our school has worked to create a way of supporting professional learning that is more personally meaningful. We were inspired by the idea of Genius Hour and how that might be relevant for teachers too. What if teachers could learn in a way that respected their individuality? What if they pursued their passions? What would that look like? How might that empower teaching and learning in our school?

We are trying to create the most powerful professional learning possible. We realize the importance of learning and growth for everyone. If we want sustainable, meaningful change in our schools, it will only happen when teachers are learning and leading.

From this thinking, we developed a plan for teachers to have greater ownership of their professional development. The idea was for teachers to pursue any learning they wanted so long as they believed it had the potential to improve our bottom line. And for schools, our bottom line is never about profits or shareholders. Our bottom line is about creating powerful learning for students.

So our message was clear. If it might make learning better for students, then pursue it. If you are passionate about it, then pursue it. That was the challenge. We asked every teacher to write a Personal Learning Plan to express a general direction for where they were headed.

The first year I met with every teacher and signed off on the plans. I quickly realized that the meetings were standing in the way of teachers pursuing their goals. In meeting after meeting, I heard questions like "Does this sound okay?" or "Is this what you were looking for?" We were seeking to empower teachers, but the requirement of a meeting and a signature seemed to take away empowerment.

So last year we didn't have the meetings or the signatures. We had several activities during our regular staff meetings to brainstorm ideas and share possibilities, and then teachers simply shared their plans through Google Classroom. We wanted to remove the barriers and get to the real work.

So much of the PD of the past felt like jumping through hoops. It wasn't always relevant to every teacher. It might be exactly what one person needed, but it might not be helpful at all for another. In a sense, it created a culture where professional learning became lifeless. It was just something that was expected and sometimes dreaded. I think some teachers began to view professional development as something that was being done to them instead of something they felt invested in.

We needed a professional development reboot, one that honors how people learn best. These principles work for students, and of course, they work for teacher-learners too.

Greater Ownership

The success or failure of each teacher's plan belongs to the individual. The responsibility for growing personally and professionally ultimately rests with the individual and not the organization. We will provide support and encouragement, but you will get out of your professional learning what you put into it.

If you are taking risks and pushing the envelope, you may experience failure in the short term, but that is okay. Sometimes we learn the most from what doesn't work. The important thing is to be invested in your own learning. We want it to be authentic and feel personal to you.

Increased Choice

Two years ago we required teachers to write goals that were aligned with certain building goals. We were emphasizing literacy since that is so important across all content areas. And we were about to launch our 1:1 program so we felt it was important to make digital tools a priority. We asked each teacher to line up their goals with the direction we were moving as a building.

But last year, we removed that requirement too. Most teachers still had goals that were very relevant to literacy or digital tools, but they had the freedom to pursue things that might only be relevant to the learning in their classroom. We trusted our teachers to choose the priorities for their learning plan. What is important to you? What will benefit your students? The choice is yours.

Providing Time

We have built-in time for teachers to collaborate and learn. Every Wednesday morning, school starts at 9:00 a.m. The late start provides time to do this work. But we still must be very careful it doesn't fill up with other stuff that leaves little time for personal learning. It's essential to try to carve out some time to allow teachers to be self-directed learners. However, time should also never be used as an excuse to not be a learner. Everyone has the same number of hours in the day, and learning is not optional for educators. We have to model the ongoing growth and lifelong learning we should seek to inspire in students.

Opportunities for Sharing

We tried to build in some opportunities for sharing Personal Learning Plans throughout the process. However, that is an area we need to continue to develop. It is so important to reflect and share in an ongoing way. Creating the structures for that is one way the school organization can support this process.

While most teachers developed and executed their plans on their own, some teachers elected to work together to create a learning team. We think it's great to allow the flexibility for teachers to choose to work independently or with others. But either way, sharing with others is essential and not optional.

Near the end of the school year, we facilitated a closing event for the Personal Learning Plans. We randomly assigned teachers to small groups for a time of sharing. Teachers were asked to bring an artifact or product from their work to share. It was a time of celebrating all the good work that was done.

What's next?

This year as we develop new learning plans, we are going to facilitate several opportunities for teachers to brainstorm and share possibilities. We want to develop more opportunities to support this work and allow staff to encourage one another and build from each other's ideas. One activity will be a First Turn/Last Turn structured dialogue. Here's how it works:

1. Groups of 6 are ideal.
2. The facilitator will ask one group member to share a possibility for their learning plan.
3. In round-robin fashion, each of the other group members will comment on the idea with no cross-talk.
4. The person who initially shared the idea will then close the round by processing his or her thinking about the comments offered by the other group members.

Emphasizing the rule that there be no cross-talk will help keep the discussion focused and on-topic. Follow-up conversations can occur after everyone has a turn in the structured dialogue.

Transformational Ideas

As I mentioned before, the criteria for the learning plan was that it had potential to improve student learning. But maybe we can aim even higher? We want to think bigger and strive to do things that don't just improve student learning but transform it.

It might be helpful for a teacher to learn how to use Powtoon, Twitter, or Glogster, but it could be transformational if the teacher learns how to use these tools to cause students to take more ownership of their learning or to create work for authentic audiences. We want to focus our energy on ideas and learning that has the potential to transform student learning. We want our work to be a game-changer for our students.

Here are a few examples of topics our teachers chose last year for the Personal Learning Plans:

- The impact of goals and journaling on student motivation
- Project Based Learning
- Nonfiction reading with IEP students
- Genius Hour with emphasis on human rights
- Formative assessment strategies
- Increased choice in demonstrating mastery
- Using CAD to create designs for 3D printing
- Developing math tutorials for student to use for review and reinforcement
- Using technology in choral rehearsals (video, music theory techniques, etc.)
- Creating "flipped classroom" lessons
- Increasing student choice in reading to develop passionate readers

I am very proud of the work our teachers have done as part of their Personal Learning Plans. We have already seen new ideas become game-changers for our school. As we continue to practice and refine this process, I believe we will see even more positive results. Ultimately, our efforts to honor teachers as learners and empower individual and collective genius have been meaningful for our school.

You're Not Reading?

With the amount of information available to educators, it is just unacceptable to continue making uninformed decisions about what works in the classroom. Never has so much information been available to improve your practice.

Take your pick. There are articles, blogs, books, social media, and more. You can connect with other educators across the globe to discuss ideas and learn from one another. And you can do it all from the comfort of your sofa right now.

And yet, there are still educators who are not growing and learning. They are still doing it the way it was when they were in school. Teaching as they were taught. They rest in their long-standing beliefs without testing them against research and new ideas.

The more professional your field, the more vital it is to read, think, and understand—to stay caught up. To stay current.

We want increased professionalism in teaching, right? We want our field to be respected. We want our profession to shine.

So we need to make sure we are contributing to the profession. We need to behave like professionals. That means we are reading the important books in our field. It means connecting with other professionals who can push us and test our ideas. And it means reflecting on how our practices align with our beliefs.

Now, give yourself a pat on the back for reading this book and pushing your own limits to reflect, grow, and learn as an educator.

It doesn't mean you're going to agree with everything you read. But if you aren't reading material that offers a viewpoint different than your own, how can you be sure of what you believe? My ideas are stronger when they are tested and hold true for me.

I realize if you are reading this book, you are probably among those who are growing and learning and moving our profession forward. You are doing the reading. You are connecting and seeking and innovating. I applaud you.

But teaching gets a bad rap. Educators are under fire. And if that is going to change, we need to do everything we can to increase the professionalism among our ranks. I urge you to share what you're reading with other teachers in your school. Use your influence to lift others up and strengthen the profession.

I believe ours is the most important profession. We need to treat it as such.

Waiting

The future-driven educator knows that it's important to take initiative and ownership. Our students are counting on us to be our best and always be improving. But some teachers are simply waiting. They aren't taking initiative or ownership of their learning. Maybe they have a fixed mindset or maybe they just don't see the need learn more. There are so many ways to learn now. It's possible to develop your skills anytime and anyplace.

In the past, professional development was something that only happened in workshops provided by the school. And so much professional development just wore teachers and administrators down. That's counterproductive.

But teachers may have gotten used to the idea that it's the school's job to provide all the professional learning. But should the school really own the burden of professional development?

I certainly think schools should support professional development, but professionals should ultimately take responsibility for their own learning. Don't wait for your school to 'develop' you. Be a learner. Getter better every day. Do things to advance your skills.

If you are constantly growing you will eventually make an impact like you never thought possible. Everyone can be successful. Find out what other successful people do and practice these skills. It's all about learning. And it's all about owning your professional growth.

Combining Twitter and Instructional Rounds

A few years ago, we started doing instructional rounds to allow teachers the opportunity to get in other teachers' classrooms. There is something very powerful about teachers observing their peers. It encourages reflection, creates awareness of the energy and feel of other classrooms in the building, and provides an opportunity to provide feedback and encouragement to colleagues. It broadens perspective.

Typically, when we do this activity we will schedule our instructional rounds to take place over a two-day period. We invite teachers to use part of their conference period on one or both days to visit other classrooms in the building. They choose where they go, how long they stay, and what type of follow-up to provide to the visits. We emphasize that the purpose of the event is to encourage one another and learn from the brief observations. We expect it will stimulate discussions about instructional practices.

In the past, we would post large sheets of paper in our commons area where teachers would write positive comments about their visits. The event built community and showed students we are interested in celebrating the learning process and sharing our classroom space with other teachers.

But then we tried something new. Instead of the paper and pen, we used Twitter to celebrate and provide feedback related to the visits. As a result of using Twitter for this purpose, a number of teachers started Twitter accounts and a few tweeted for the first time. I emailed resources about Twitter in advance and gave teachers a few ideas of things to look for in their visits. We used our own hashtag to tag our posts so everyone could follow.

Give the Gift of Reading

Since professional reading is so important, we decided to get every teacher a book for Christmas. It was a way to show appreciation and provide something valuable and helpful. I developed a list with about a dozen possibilities. Our teachers picked a selection from the list. Several of the titles were education books and several were related to psychology, success, or performance but certainly relatable to educators' professional work.

The response was incredible. Our teachers were so grateful for the books. It was an honor to present them at our final meeting before the semester break and thank them for what they do for kids and thank them for always continuing to learn and grow.

Every day educators can make a difference for students. You will never know the full extent of your impact. But you have a big responsibility too. You must continue to learn. You must model learning for your students. And you must ensure that you are becoming the best you can be. Your ability to impact the future is directly correlated to your willingness to continue to learn. Never stop reading. Never stop growing.

CHAPTER 10

Learn, Unlearn, Relearn

In Moscow, there are about 35,000 stray dogs loose in the city. Most of them were let out on the street by owners who didn't want them anymore for one reason or another. For every 300 people living in Moscow, there is one stray dog. It's a tough life on the streets, but the dogs have adapted to their surroundings, relying on their wolf-like instincts to survive.[1]

These wild dogs are scavengers and beggars. Many of the dogs have actually learned to read human body language and assess which people are most likely to give them food. Some have even learned to ride the subway to travel to other locations in the city that are most suitable for receiving a meal. Yes, these strays are hopping rides on the subway system. The dogs are pack animals as you might expect, but rather than the biggest or strongest being the alpha or leader, that position is held by the cleverest dog in the pack. *It takes a smart dog to survive in a complex world.*

In Search of Better Thinking, Not Right Answers

Knowing right answers is not enough.

The future will demand problem solving and adaptability. Content is driving too much of what we do, not learning. Knowing content makes you informed. Knowing how to learn anything makes you indispensable. The content will change and the answers won't be the same, but the ability to learn and adapt is timeless. In the past, school has been all about right answers. In the future, it needs to be all about better thinking.

Consider this question: what if we thought more about how we would learn something ourselves and less about how we are going to teach it? If you were going to set out to learn a topic, apart from the formal school setting, what would you do? How would you learn if it was completely up to you? The purpose of school, after all, is learning, not teaching. How would you learn if it was completely up to you? I'm guessing it would probably include using technology, finding resources, connecting with experts, etc.

Our students learn so much from the internet. That is how they learn. I know online learning is invaluable to me, even beyond professional learning. I've learned how to solve problems in my garden. How to fix my vacuum cleaner. How to self-publish a book. If you learn something for yourself, you will remember it much longer than if someone teaches it to you in the traditional sense.

What we learn for ourselves, we learn forever.

Ready for the Unexpected

Too often we give children answers to know rather than problems to solve. —Roger Lewin

If students are going to be adaptable learners, they must be ready to apply skills to situations they have never seen before. It's tough to practice for the unpredictable. What do our students need to be ready for anything?

1. Students should be working with interesting questions and authentic problems.
2. They should be doing the work of professionals; the kinds of things real world professionals do.
3. They should not learn content in isolation. Unless you can do something with your knowledge, it isn't that useful.

We always need to remember the goal of school is to transfer skills. The purpose of school is not to be good at school. The purpose of an education is to help students succeed in life outside of school.

Learning for life is the heart of all we do.

Google Doesn't Have Answers

The need to know the capital of Florida died when my phone learned the answer. Rather the students of tomorrow need to be able to think creatively. They will need to learn on their own, adapt to new challenges, and innovate on the fly. —Anthony Chivetta

Information is abundant. Far more abundant than at any time in history and that has changed everything. By the year 2020, there will be about 6 billion connected devices on the planet, each of these with the ability to access the sum of human knowledge.

But Google still doesn't have the answers to the most interesting questions. And it can't solve our most pressing problems.

It's only possible to develop answers to the most compelling, worthwhile questions through good thinking. And solving the most pressing problems only happens by applying what you know. Google cannot do our thinking for us.

What kinds of questions are you asking in your classroom? Ones that students can look up answers on Google. Or ones that require gathering information, making sense of it, recognizing patterns, considering various possibilities, and ultimately developing extraordinary solutions.

Meaning is Made, Not Just Accepted.

We've been talking about Bloom's Taxonomy and critical thinking for as long as I've been an educator. And yet we still have work to do to get kids cognitively engaged in classrooms.

We can't seem to shake the traditional methods that turn education into a delivery system, rather than a powerful engine of discovery and inquiry.

So much of conventional wisdom is wrong. For instance, many teachers believe we should teach the basics and then if we have time, include opportunities for critical thinking. Our assessments are often organized that way. Most of the items will be recall/knowledge level questions with one or two performance events or critical thinking tasks at the end. It seems like critical thinking is always an afterthought.

In my first year of teaching, I remember one of my mentors gave me this advice, "Make them (the students) think." And that's exactly what we need to do. We need to design learning that involves students in making meaning, not just accepting information. If we want students to get a deeper understanding and enjoy learning, that is what we must do.

Delivery System	Discovery System
Students are expected to accept information (textbook, lecture, study packet, notes, etc).	Students are making meaning of information (thinking critically and creatively).
Learning is impersonal and disconnected.	It connects to the learner's interest, aptitude, experience, and even their personality.
Understanding is limited to what was taught.	Understanding often results in new ideas.
The teacher is doing much of the thinking and explaining.	The student is forced to assume more cognitive load.
Learning is measured by right and wrong answers.	Learning is measured by the quality of your thinking (and ultimately quality thinking will result in right answers).
The teacher mostly decides the direction of learning.	The students' questions help determine the direction of the learning.
Teaches step-by-step problem solving (at best).	Teaches students to activate their reasoning skills to solve problems.
Relies on compliance, following instructions, rules.	Relies on curiosity, interests, and exploration.
Passive, receiving, accepting, memorizing type of learning.	Active, reasoning, questioning, connecting, synthesizing type of learning.

There are numerous advantages to discovery learning. Students will remember more of the facts and fundamentals of the discipline when they learn this way. They will have more context to connect ideas and make learning stick. They will also develop skills as independent learners, something that will serve them well their whole life.

And it doesn't have to be complicated. Although I'm a big fan of project-based learning, we can make students think in simple ways without an extended project. Sometimes the simplest teacher moves are the most effective.

Try this: Wait longer after you ask a question before you accept a student answer. Then, wait longer after the student responds to the question before you say anything. Instead of saying the answer is right or wrong, ask, "And why do you think that?"

Design for Thinking

I'll never forget the advice the ponytail teacher gave me in my first year of teaching: "Make them think." That's always stuck with me. No matter what we do in the classroom we should design teaching for the cognitive moment. Make the students think. Always seek to push thinking just a little deeper. Work to ask more interesting questions.

As I visit classrooms and observe teaching and learning, I see teachers asking lots of questions. But too often, the questions don't require sustained thought. Sometimes they are just a way for the teacher to make the lesson delivery seem a little more interactive, to keep students on their toes. But the questions don't require elaboration or explanation. Mostly, this type of questioning is fact checking. Do students know the facts?

But when the questions require deeper thought, the entire classroom has a different feeling. There is a kind of tension. It's not a bad tension. It's not tension about if the answer is right or wrong. It's about understanding, making meaning, and thinking about different perspectives.

One of our teachers is constantly pushing for the cognitive moment. He really makes students think. I would almost describe it as interrogation, but he interrogates in a way that's safe. He doesn't shine bright lights in their eyes or anything like that. **He presses with questions to arrive at understanding,**

not just a right answer. Almost all these questions are *how* or *why* questions. And they require answers that are more than a couple words or phrases. Students are learning how to communicate their ideas.

And participation is not optional. If we only ask students who raise their hands to answer a question, only about a third of students will ever participate. If I were back in the classroom as a teacher, I would work to establish a culture of cold calling. I would not ask students to raise their hands to answer a question. I would randomly call on students, or use a method like a random name generator to determine who will respond. Of course, I would also work to create a kind of safety in that. I would give students think time before calling on someone. And I would try to use every response as an opportunity for more thinking, even if it didn't seem reasonable. Dylan Wiliam (@dylanwiliam) has written about this idea. He calls for teachers to create classrooms where students raise their hands not to answer a question but only to ask a question.[2]

Wicked Problem

While working on my doctorate at the University of Missouri, we were assigned teams and required to analyze and address a ridiculously complex case study appropriately named the Wicked Problem. When I recently attended a reunion banquet, the Wicked Problem was something we all recounted. It left a lasting impression. It was something every doctoral student in educational leadership was faced with. We spent hours thinking about this problem, researching possible solutions, and coming to a consensus about our ideas. It was an incredibly authentic project. It was high stakes. It culminated in an extensive research paper and a presentation to the doctoral faculty.

The Wicked Problem forced us to work together with our team to develop a 25-page solution. Because of the complexity, it was impossible to just hand off different parts of the assignment and work separately. We had to work interdependently. Our solutions would be dependent on how well we could work together and make our collective thinking stronger than any of us could be on our own. Some of the teams almost killed each other during this process. There are a lot of high achievers and strong personalities in a doctoral program.

But our group functioned efficiently and productively, for the most part. There was give and take and a willingness to share leadership at different times. It was a valuable experience. Our students also need to have experiences like this. They need to solve problems that require sustained thought, positive interdependence, and teamwork to succeed.

Better Writing, Better Thinking

No matter how the world changes, students will benefit from writing to learn. Kids need to write. In fact, every person who is interested in reaching his potential must write. Writing is a powerful engine of growth. As author and journalist Bill Wheeler observed, "Good writing is clear thinking made visible." But writing doesn't just make thinking visible. Writing also informs our thinking. It works both ways. When we write, our thinking is made stronger. And with better thinking, we are made better writers.

Traditionally, writing was taught in English class, and the 5-paragraph essay was the ultimate expression of a student writer. But writing shouldn't just happen in English class, and the 5-paragraph essay is like nothing that is written in the real world. Authentic writing is rarely 5-paragraphs with an opening thesis, and topical sentences, and supporting details. More authentic writing will happen when students are consistently practicing writing across every discipline and for a variety of purposes.

We must aim to help students see themselves as writers. That won't happen for all students if it's limited to English class.

When Lori's health forced her to stop working as an itinerant teacher, I encouraged her to start blogging. I had been blogging for a couple of years, and I believed in the value of establishing and sharing a voice online. She still writes regularly at http://www.lorigeurin.com/ about her passions—health, wellness, and helping others with Lyme disease.

She sees herself as a writer now. Sometimes she even complains about not having enough time to write. Wouldn't it be great if our schools had a culture of writing with that level of passion and commitment? Wouldn't it be great if our students wished for more opportunities to write? What future opportunities would our students enjoy if they developed a writing identity while in school?

New Dorp High School in Staten Island credits a focus on writing with completely turning the school around. Brockton High School in Brockton, Massachusetts has a similar story. Both schools were among the worst performing in their states. Both faced significant challenges with highly diverse student populations, low-income families, and labels as failing schools. Both developed a relentless focus on writing across all content areas.

At Brockton, the expectation was students writing in every class, every period, every day. New Dorp had similar expectations and taught students analytical strategies to support writing and thinking. The results for both schools were extraordinary. Student achievement skyrocketed, graduation rates soared, and the learning cultures of both schools were greatly strengthened.

The Expert

What is more valuable—to be an expert or a learner? Or an expert learner? Since information was scarce in a time before the age of the internet, the expert had the market cornered. There was only one way to learn XYZ and that was from the experts in the field of XYZ. Experts held an intellectual primacy that was irrefutable. But knowledge is multiplying. And quite literally by the hour, there is so much more to know. In the 1980's, Buckminster Fuller theorized the "Knowledge Doubling Curve."

He noticed that until 1900 human knowledge doubled approximately every century. By the end of World War II, knowledge was doubling every 25 years. Today things are not as simple as different types of knowledge have different rates of growth. For example, nanotechnology knowledge is doubling every two years and clinical knowledge every 18 months. But on average human knowledge is doubling every 13 months. According to IBM, the build out of the "internet of things" will lead to the doubling of knowledge every 12 hours.[3]

As knowledge continues to rapidly increase, it becomes increasingly impossible for experts to know all there is to know. In any field, it will be essential to be ready to learn more at all times. It will be critical to have the mindset of a learner. It will be necessary to always continue learning. As a result, the idea of the teacher as the content expert must be retooled.

It's great when the teacher is the content expert, but it's even more valuable when the teacher is the learning expert. Content is changing so fast it's impossible to keep up. The only way to thrive is to be a forever-learner.

Being a learner is more valuable than being a student; being a student is temporary but learning lasts forever. Teachers who recognize this will be able to help prepare students for this increasing complexity. They will help their students learn how to learn. They will not just be concerned with what to learn, but how to learn will be a chief aim.

Think Like an Innovator

Like many educators, I'm excited about the discussion of innovation in schools. It's great to think about how education is changing to meet the needs of today's learners. I am convinced that we can solve any problem that comes our way if we are committed to better thinking. Innovation starts with understanding a current reality and then developing and implementing ideas that have the potential to create positive change.

Here are 7 strategies educators can use to think like an innovator.

1. Practice Creative Thinking

Creative thinking is closely tied to innovation. When I think of invention or innovation, I think of creativity. Some seem to think creativity is an elusive, inborn trait. They throw up their hands, "Well I'm just not very creative." But I believe creativity is more about being willing to take a risk, to try something new, to make mistakes, and to try again.

Thomas Edison is perhaps the greatest inventor in history, holding 1,093 patents. His inventions changed the world. But Edison recognized that his ability to create was a result of his perseverance. He just never gave up on ideas. He would come at it another way until he found something that worked.

I haven't failed. I've just found 10,000 ways that won't work.
—Thomas Edison

2. Embrace Reflective Thinking

Reflective thinking is so important to learning and growing. Through careful observation, you can better understand the current reality and build on it through reflection. Reflection is revisiting the past to gain clarity and understanding. Innovation is not just following the latest fads in education. It is considering the current way, how it might improve, and reflecting on how new ideas might benefit your school. You can gain perspective and learn from the mistakes of the past by reflecting.

We don't learn from experience. We learn from reflecting on experience. —John Dewey

3. Develop Strategic Thinking

Innovation may seem lofty and idealistic but it still involves strategy and planning. Strategy helps to give you direction for today and for the future. It helps you think about where you're headed, what you will need to get there, and how long it will take. Innovation without strategic thinking won't go anywhere. You might have innovative ideas, but you will need planning and action to move them forward. As Henry Ford said, "Nothing is particularly hard if you divide it into smaller parts."

4. Engage in Collaborative Thinking

If you want to develop the best ideas, test your thoughts with the best thinkers you know. Isolation rarely results in better ideas. A good idea becomes a great one when you receive feedback, even from those who have completely different thoughts from your own. A high-performing, collaborative team can achieve compounding results from testing ideas and building on one another's collective genius. Collaboration is a powerful accelerator of innovation.

Coming together is success: keeping together is progress; working together is success. —Henry Ford

5. Activate Big Picture Thinking

Big picture thinking has no limitations. All the assumptions about the problem are set aside. Big picture thinking is daring to dream. It's getting cozy with ambiguity. It often involves thinking about ideas that might seem unrelated and applying what is known to new contexts.

Earlier in *Future Driven*, I considered the question, *"What if schools were more like Google or Starbucks."* I was thinking big, beyond the normal ways we think about education. Is it possible to apply some of the principles of today's leading companies to our work in schools? Big picture thinking goes far beyond what is commonplace.

> *Whatever the mind can conceive and believe, it can achieve.*
> *—Napoleon Hill*

6. Believe in Possibility Thinking

Possibility thinkers believe that even the most difficult problems can be solved. The focus is not on why something can't be done; instead, possibility thinking asks why not? One of the surest ways to stifle a great idea is to start thinking too quickly about how it can be done. Start with why it should be done, and then enlist possibility thinkers to figure out how to make it happen.

A great example of possibility thinking was conveyed in the film, *The Martian*. Matt Damon plays an astronaut mistakenly presumed dead and left behind on Mars. Survival on Mars is not an easy thing and chances of rescue are slim. It will be four years before the next mission arrives.

Damon's character does not give up, however. He begins to look for possibilities to gain hope for survival. He says you must solve one problem, and then the next problem, and then the next. And "if you solve enough problems, you get to go home." Ultimately, possibility thinking on his part, and on the part of others, results in his unlikely rescue.

7. Don't Neglect Purposeful Thinking

Some innovations almost happen by accident. By implementing innovative thinking, new ideas may result in unexpected findings. For example, Post-It Notes were invented at 3M when a new adhesive wasn't all that sticky and was initially considered useless. But when someone had the idea to apply the new formula to a different kind of notepad, a new office staple was born, almost by accident.

But many innovations are not this random. More purposeful thinking can be very helpful in schools. What outcomes do you want for students? Begin with the end in mind. Do you want to engage learners, improve student ownership, develop critical thinking, or increase understanding? Do you want better readers and writers? Then be purposeful to try new ideas that have the potential to improve these outcomes. Purposeful innovation turns ideas into results. Our activities and goals must be consistent with the results we want to achieve.

CHAPTER 11

Community and Beyond

I arrived at my office bright and early as usual, but I immediately noticed something was different. There was a handwritten sticky note posted at my door, "Make a new friend" with a smiley face drawn underneath the message.

It was going to be one of the most positive starts we ever had at BHS. Every student, in every classroom, would start their day with a note of encouragement. You matter. Love yourself. Give someone a hug. You're an amazing person. Smile. Give someone a compliment and tweet it.

Our Character Council is a group of students who work to help build a positive school culture. They spent hours writing these little notes and placing them on desks and tables in every classroom. So every student would arrive at school to find a handwritten note of encouragement.

Students began sharing these on Twitter and Instagram using the hashtag #StartsWithUs. The positive vibe was being shared with others. Because positive vibes are like that. They are contagious. When you choose to share the best of you with others, either online or in person, it helps make the world a better place.

We get to choose our attitude each day. Our attitude determines more about how our day will go than anything else. But our attitude also contributes to how other people will experience their day too. We live in community. We impact others.

Our school is like a family. Our choices ripple out and influence others. Lifting up others builds a strong community.

So how is your attitude today? Are you committing to bring the best version of you to your school or classroom? *If everyone in your school had your attitude, what kind of place would it be?*

We are facing challenges around the globe with how we interact. Life is busier. We are all in a hurry. People are crowded together in cities. Social media is filled with negative vibes. Many of us are worried about the future.

The need for stronger communities is important to our future, locally and globally. We need to know each other, help each other, and most importantly understand each other. Schools need to help bring down the walls and connect with our local community and with communities far away. We have so many opportunities to bring people together, and we can't allow school to be set apart from the real world.

Overcoming Isolation

With the digital tools that have emerged in the last decade, we are more connected than ever before. We can connect practically anywhere, anytime, with just about anyone. It's easy to keep up with friends, family, and our entire network through social media platforms like Facebook, Twitter, SnapChat, Instagram, and more. We can talk with someone like we're in the same room via Skype or Google Hangouts. It seems like just about every moment of our lives is documented on social media and shared with someone.

And yet it seems like people are struggling with loneliness like never before. It's normal for all of us to feel lonely from time to time, but when you're stuck in these feelings of loneliness that's a serious problem. Chronic loneliness is on the rise. And it's possible our culture of hyper-connectivity is part of the problem. One study found that people who spent more time on social media actually reported more feelings of loneliness. You see happy pictures of other people having fun, spending time together, and celebrating success, and you think you're missing out. You don't think you have as many friends, you're not as interesting, or you don't measure up.[1]

But technology isn't the problem. The problem is related to how we interact with one another and how we invest in relationships. All the platforms we have for connecting can be useful if we leverage them as a way to support our personal, face-to-face relationships. When social media replaces real-world relationships, there is cause for concern. When it's about gathering likes and follows, it reveals an emptiness. When social media is an attempt to fill a void, it's detrimental to a person's well-being.

Global Learning

Today, we are easily able to make connections around the world. Through the power of technology, the world is shrinking. Things that happen on the other side of the planet can have implications for our stories as well. We are truly interconnected. We are joined by markets, global politics, environmental issues and more. Many of the most relevant problems of our time are global problems.

As a result, it is important for students to have opportunities for learning that connects beyond the school walls. Our students need to get a sense that they are part of a much larger story. To create the future leaders and problem-solvers, we must help students understand how they have a place in a global society. Students need to see themselves as global citizens

Darren Ellwein's (@dellwein) middle school students in South Dakota have experienced learning that connects far beyond their school. They've learned in collaboration with students in Norway after Darren connected with educator Terje Pedersen (@terjepe) from Norway via Twitter. This partnership resulted in a variety of shared learning experience across continents. The students reviewed each other's writing, learned about Native Americans and stereotypes, and used Spheros for coordinate plane learning in math.

We've made global connections in our school too. But sometimes I think we make it too hard. It needs to be more routine. Maybe we think it has to fit perfectly into our curriculum. Maybe we don't think we have time. But it only takes a moment to connect. It only takes a few keystrokes to send a message. We must share our schools with the world and tell our stories. And hear their stories. That's the only way we'll build more understanding. And that's probably as important as any of the curriculum we're teaching today.

Beyond the Classroom

When I was in high school, 1 was required to take a full year of speech as a graduation requirement. For the first semester, the course was like a traditional public-speaking course. We developed and presented a variety of speeches. It was certainly a positive experience. The fear of public speaking is well-documented, and this was a good growth opportunity for me.

But the thing I remember most about the course was the second semester, where our class was entirely project-based. Everyone in the class was assigned to a team, and we worked to develop and produce a newscast on local closed-circuit cable TV. Our school had a TV production studio and each week we produced a full broadcast with anchors, reporters, producers, camera operators, studio technicians, etc. Pretty cool, don't you think?

When our project team was assigned to develop a feature story about a topic that was important to our community, we did a piece on illegal dump sites in our area. We could leave school to go take video footage of some of the places people were illegally dumping trash. We interviewed law enforcement and other community leaders about the problem. The learning experience was incredibly authentic, ahead of its time in so many ways.

Our mentor through the entire process was Mr. England, our teacher. He was an incredible educator. The entire course was developed under his leadership. I think there are several reasons it was so effective. **First, it was a project that was real. We were doing things that professionals in the field actually do.** It involved community. We felt like our story was important because it involved a real problem that needed to be addressed. There was a chance of failure, but also recognition of success. Our work would be shared with a real audience in our community, so if we didn't meet our deadline or we produced a poor segment, it was completely on us.

So what are the barriers that are keeping schools from providing more authentic learning opportunities, like what I've described?

We are time-bound and standards-driven. If we are going to offer more authenticity in learning we must embed standards in the learning, but not let the standards drive the learning. Some of the best learning experiences may not correlate to higher scores on standardized tests. We have to establish priorities that don't place test scores ahead of authentic learning experiences.

Our students can't or won't learn this way. It's hard for some teachers to trust that students will succeed when given the option to fail. In a compliance-driven culture, teachers hold more control over instruction, and it's hard to think about allowing students to drive more of the learning. It will require some serious work on the front-end to help students take on greater commitment and responsibility. They have been used to being "spoon-fed" for most of their years in school.

Our school can't afford the technology. Although technology is not a requirement for authentic learning experiences, it does help. Certainly, not every school has the resources to provide a fully functional television studio. But even a cheap smartphone device that is several years old can be used to research, create, and assist in the development of authentic learning opportunities.

One of the benefits of Mr. England's class was the opportunity to learn outside the classroom. We could leave school to work on our project. I remember how weird it felt (and how great) to be away from campus for part of our school work. Students can't always leave school to work on projects, but I do think there is value in moving learning beyond the classroom walls.

Significant Learning

Don't ask a student what she wants to be when she grows up. Ask her what problem she wants to solve...then give her the environment to build the knowledge, skills, and abilities she needs to solve that problem. —Jaime Casap

So how was school today? Fine.

What did you do? Nothing.

What did you learn? Blank stare.

What problem did you solve? I'm guessing that question doesn't get asked very often around the dinner table. But shouldn't school work involve solving real problems?

Too much of what happens in school doesn't seem to connect to anything in our students' lives right now. It doesn't give the sense that this matters beyond getting a grade or pleasing the teacher or progressing toward graduation. And so, when asked about their day in school, it's no wonder that students really don't have much to say.

I think most students and many teachers have a limited view of where learning happens. When they think of where you get your education, it's at a school building. But to me, the school is more about the people than the place. It's more about the experience than the location. I think students would find their education more personally meaningful if it connected beyond the school walls. For many students, real life happens only happens outside of school. Then, they leave the real world to step into the halls of the school, a place that doesn't really connect with their lives and interests.

That's why it's so important to take the school to the community and bring the community into the school. Or to go beyond the local community and go places far and wide. Learning isn't confined to a place. Let's take it with us wherever we go.

Conflict

Worldwide, people are living closer together than ever before. About 81% of Americans live in urban areas. The U.S. continues to be increasingly urban. There are over 500 cities in America with populations of 1 million or greater. In 1950, there were only 83 cities in the world with populations exceeding one million; by 2007, this number had risen to 468. Imagine life in a megacity. These population centers have more than 10 million each. These are enormous cities like Tokyo, Japan with over 33 million or San Paulo, Brazil at nearly 18 million.

Imagine the traffic jams. Imagine the congestion. Imagine the sewage system. Imagine if the sewage system is lacking. Makes me thankful for my small town of 10,000!

But not only are people living closer together. We are also living closer to people who are different from us. Or, we are brought closer to people who are different to us through our connected, online, media-infused world. Cultures are literally colliding. People with different beliefs, different cultures, and different ideas are all sharing this relatively small planet. There is going to be conflict. How do we handle it? What will the future look like?

The collision of cultures creates anxiety and stress. There is bound to be conflict. You don't have to look very far to find conflict in this world.

It's important for our students to learn to be understanding of people who are different. Empathy is such an important skill in a pluralistic society. We must recognize that our neighbors are not just the ones who are like us, or even who live close to us. Our neighbors are each person who resides on the planet.

Social media has revealed the loss of civility in contemporary life. Even officials in the highest offices, ones in greatest positions of influence, are setting a poor example of how to interact with others in dignified, positive, productive ways.

Some people criticize social media or avoid it entirely because of the negative aspects. But I don't believe that is the best approach. Social media is not going away. Our students need to learn how to use it positively. They will benefit from seeing the examples of caring adults in their networks. The negative aspect will always be there, but we need to do our best to overcome the bad with the good. We need leaders to be upstanders and not bystanders. We need examples of positive responses to overcome the negative voices.

I was very proud of how our students responded to a negative social media incident this past year in our school. Actually, there have been several similar examples to this one. Someone made a negative comment about our front office secretaries on Twitter using our school hashtag. Of course, it's not right to criticize someone like that publicly. But our secretaries are amazing and caring so it was especially rude and untrue. A bunch of students saw the negative tweet and started posting positive things about the secretaries, how nice they are, how helpful, how much they appreciate them. It really turned a negative into a positive rather quickly.

Maslow vs. Bloom

It's clear that students who don't have basic needs met struggle to focus on learning. When I hear stories from our students of the things they are dealing with in their life away from school, I am amazed they function as well as they do. I'm amazed they show up at all. I've been humbled to think of the circumstances our students must endure and overcome. They are overcomers.

But typically, when a student's basic physical and emotional needs aren't being met, it's tough to learn effectively. In our district, we are blessed to have a program called *Care to Learn*. It was started in our area a few years ago by Doug Pitt, a local philanthropist also known as the brother of Brad Pitt. You probably know him from the grocery checkout lane.

Care to Learn provides for the emergent health, hunger, and hygiene needs of students. Any teacher can refer a student to receive support from this program. There's almost zero red tape. Our counselors can instantly access funds to meet needs like clothing, shoes, food, eyeglasses, etc. They also keep a fully stocked food pantry in our school, and we regularly send students home with food. We've benefited from *Care to Learn* over and again to help meet basic needs for our students.

A portion of the proceeds from the sale of *Future Driven* will go to support the *Care to Learn* fund in our community. It was important to me for this book to do something good for our students.[2]

Going Places

Learning takes you places. The more you'll learn, the more places you'll go.

Learning is filled with adventures. There are so many things to see. There is so much to learn.

As a kid, I remember charging across a battlefield, exploring a cave, and being awestruck at the tomb of King Tutankhamun in the presence of an ancient mummy. In reality, I wasn't at the tomb, and I'm not sure it was King Tut, but I did have the opportunity as a kid to see a mummy at a museum on a school trip. It was pretty cool.

It's great to go places to explore and learn.

As I look back on my school experience, these trips away from school were extremely valuable. They brought learning to life. But they didn't bring the mummy back to the life. Unfortunately, none of the trips I took were quite like *Night at the Museum*.

Students at Bolivar High School have unbelievable opportunities to travel and learn. For over 60 years, every senior class has traveled to Washington, D.C. More recently, we've added New York City to that experience.

Students visit the National Mall, the Smithsonian, the Holocaust Museum, and Arlington National Cemetery, and more.

I like to go along on our senior trip every chance I get. One of the things that is most powerful is the Changing of the Guard at the Tomb of the Unknown Soldier. Each year, four of our student body officers participate in a Wreath Laying Ceremony. It brings such meaning and significance to think we are connected to remembering soldiers who gave the ultimate sacrifice for the freedom we enjoy.

Never take freedom for granted. It provides us with unbelievable opportunities. It's an opportunity to go places. It's an opportunity to learn.

Together

The future-driven leader recognizes the importance of teamwork. People are stronger when they work together, share ideas, and borrow insights from the knowledge and experience of others.

Individual success is an outgrowth of team success. No one ever accomplished anything without help from others. Isolation is not helpful. Isolation is a protector of the status quo and a killer of innovation. It hampers growth. Connect with your students, your colleagues, the custodians, the cooks, the community. Don't get absorbed in your own little world and forget about the people who need you. You can learn and grow from each person you meet.

Teamwork is about togetherness. It is about relying on the strengths of each person. It's about sharing goals and wanting the best for your teammates.

Individual success is an outgrowth of team success. No one ever accomplished anything without help from others.
#FutureDriven

I know our school has a positive culture when I see teachers and students genuinely happy for one another's success. We should always cheer each other on. I see teachers going above and beyond every day to help each other succeed. And to help their students succeed. We should *seek* to cooperate and lift each other up.

Every person in a school can be a leader by giving of themselves for the success of others.

Partners

Our school enjoys strong community partnerships that provide an excellent network of support for our students, teachers, and programs. Recently, we began developing a computer science program, including a dual credit course through our local university, which just happens to have an award-winning computer science program. The university provided training for our teacher and was a valuable resource in the development of our curriculum. We also offer 19 other dual credit courses, which allows our students to get a significant head start on college.

We are blessed by a community education foundation that supports the school with education grants and scholarships for our students. Local businesses, like our hospital, have supported our health occupations and culinary arts programs, among others. One of our local banks donates 5 cents of every debit card purchase to the schools, generating thousands in funds for various projects.

Our local Rotary Club sponsors a student civic organization in our school, Interact. They also invite two seniors every month to attend their meetings as Student Rotarians. And, they recognize our outstanding academic achievers at a banquet each year.

There are many more examples of how our community partners make our school stronger. How are you reaching out to your community to offer them a chance to help? There are people who want to support your classroom or school. Build those relationships. When the community has the chance to work in partnership with the school, everyone wins.

Extreme Classroom Makeover

Wouldn't it be great if every classroom was an incredible space for learning? If we are going to pursue excellence, it should be in every area, including how our school looks. As a community partnership activity, we've invited groups to take a classroom and work with a teacher to do an extreme classroom makeover. It's kind of like the shows that used to be popular. In a couple of days, a group of volunteers completely transform a classroom. They paint it, and add design elements, anything that will make it stand out in an awesome way.

I look forward to partnering with more groups in our community to transform more classrooms. Of course, the teacher must be open to the idea. And there are some logistics to work out. But it's a great way to invite the community to contribute.

Service Learning

We also think it's important for our students to give back to the community. Many clubs and organizations are consistently volunteering time and making an impact in outreach. This past year we also had a community service day for all sophomores. One of our counselors led this entire project as part of her personal learning plan. We got the idea from another school in our area. It was awesome!

Our students went to about a dozen different sites to help nonprofits and service organizations with various projects. They spent the entire day painting, pulling weeds, playing games with senior citizens, and sorting donations at a thrift store. We finished the day with some reflection, celebration, and ice cream sandwiches. We were excited about this event and look forward to doing it again.

We have a group at Bolivar High School known as the SWAT team. SWAT stands for Students Working to Advance Technology. The club started in 2015 to support our 1:1 program that was just getting off the ground.

SWAT provides valuable support related to how we use technology in our school. For instance, they have presented how-to workshops for teachers during our annual PD day, the past two years. And they've been involved in parent open house to demonstrate ways technology is being used for learning in our school. They also help students in the library with their Chromebooks.

Most recently, the group offered tech support for senior citizens in our community on Thursdays after school. We publicized the opportunity in our local newspaper and on Facebook. It was a simple concept. We had some digital natives (our students) on hand to help the older crowd in our community with tech related questions.

The senior adults could bring their own device (most of them did) or the students used their Chromebooks to help with Facebook, Gmail, or whatever tool they wanted to learn.

We didn't really know what to expect. It was our first time trying something like this. But it was a huge success. We had customers every single Thursday, and several of our guests came back week after week. It was helpful to the senior citizens we served. It was a fantastic opportunity to connect with our community. And it was a great learning experience for our students, too.

Professionals Advise

Each week as part of Senior Seminar, we have career professionals from our community visit BHS for our Liberators Learn speaking series. They share information, provide advice, and answer student questions related to their specific career field. We've had dozens of community members participate in this program. Senior Seminar also provides job shadowing and community service opportunities for our seniors.

The purpose of Senior Seminar is to help students prepare for the transition to whatever they will do after high school. Of course, we highly encourage students to go beyond high school for additional education either at a 2-year or 4-year university.

The great thing about Liberators Learn is that it brings people into our school with real world experience. These are some of the most successful people in our community sharing wisdom and career advice with our students.

CHAPTER 12

Digital Matters

All technology hovers between being a blessing and a burden. It makes life simpler and more complex at the same time. We've all seen how things can go wrong.

Years ago, when I first started using Twitter, my smartphone was not all that smart and the quickest way for me to post a Tweet was by SMS. You can still do this. You connect your mobile number to Twitter and when they receive a text message from your number they post it to your feed. When texting, you just want to make sure you are sending your message to the right number.

Lori and I had an argument the night before. I had been less than the best version of me. I owed her an apology. I arrived at school early and wanted to reach out to her to smooth it over. Sounds like a smart move on my part, right? Only, I sent the message to Twitter by accident. So, my private apology to my wife went out for everyone to see. I only realized it when one of my teachers came rushing into my office thinking I might not have meant to post my message to social media.

She was right.

I quickly deleted the message and have taken some ribbing for the incident ever since. I will never forget all the smiles from students that day at school. "Hey, I saw your tweet this morning, Dr. G!" Or, they would just grin and give me thumbs up. Of course, my wife thought all of this was a riot. What could be a better finish to a marital conflict than an apology and public humiliation?

This example was ultimately a harmless way tech can go wrong. But technology has significant challenges that are not so easily dismissed. It can be a distraction, a danger, and a time-waster. We can become addicted to screens. Technology can fail when you need it most, like when you've planned that awesome 'digital' lesson and the Wi-Fi goes down. It can have a negative impact on our social skills and how we interact with others.

The internet is a dangerous place that requires good judgment and a set of skills to navigate successfully.

The Best and the Worst

At its worst, technology reveals the dark and depraved aspects of our humanity. It's a place filled with hate and harm. Almost everyone has been touched by technology in some sort of harmful way. Left unchecked, technology can lead to isolation, depression, loss of privacy, loss of sexual boundaries, increased bullying, and more. As I reflect on all the negatives of technology use, it's easy for me to understand why some people don't like technology.

In schools, technology comes with many of the same problems. And the constant potential for distractions and the loss of attention span have to be considerations for educators.

Yes, there are many obstacles to overcome in using technology in schools in productive ways. But do we really have a choice if we want to prepare students for their futures? Won't technology only play an increasing role in life and work? If school is the only place in their lives students don't use technology, won't that make the experience even less relevant for them?

Despite the challenges, there are many possibilities with technology. Some people only see the problems. Others see the possibilities.

I think we need more possibility thinking in education. Technology has opened up all sorts of new opportunities for learning in our school. It's helped our students and teachers link with the community through social media; we've celebrated learning, connected with experts, created all sorts of amazing content, and shared our work far beyond the walls of our school.

The Resistance

I don't like technology. I'm not good at it. It's not a priority. I don't feel confident with it. If it's really that important, kids will figure it out some other place.

And maybe they will. Maybe.

Technology may not be your thing. You may not feel confident with it. You may wish that it wasn't so important. But it is because it allows you to leverage your skills. It opens doors of opportunity. So even if you wish it would just go away, it won't.

I'm not good with technology.

I'm not good at reading.

I'm not good at learning.

I'm not good at making copies of worksheets.

Well, that last one would be okay by me.

Do We Really Have Time for Digital Citizenship?

We started a series of weekly discussions in our building about life in our increasingly digital world. I guess you could call it Digital Citizenship. I prefer to call it Digital Leadership. We have a half-hour academic support time built into our schedule four days a week. We provided teachers with a couple of choices for activities that were easy to implement. We showed video clips with our own students sharing some thoughts about how their digital life impacts their overall life. And then we discussed the upsides and downsides to technology, for us personally, for our relationships, and even for our nation.

In my visits to classrooms, there were lively discussions during this time. These are relevant issues that kids really want to discuss. They want to hear different ideas, share their experience, and wrestle with how to successfully navigate this complex world.

But there were also some challenges to making this happen. Our teachers and students are accustomed to having this academic support time for tutoring, making up missed work, and other important tasks. There were some legitimate concerns where the loss of the time was going to impact the academics of students. They really needed to retake that quiz or there was a study session for a test the next day. And so, I let the teachers decide. If you feel the academic need is pressing, then skip the Digital Leadership lesson this time.

Even my daughter, Maddie, was disappointed she couldn't use that time for academics. She is playing tennis and has missed a ton of school for matches and tournaments. She's working hard to get caught up and values Liberator Time to get stuff done.

As I've thought about how this has all played out, my biggest question concerns our priorities. Are we really paying attention to our students' needs? There is no question that preparing students academically is important. But if we aren't preparing students for life in a world that is rapidly changing, will the academic knowledge really be that helpful?

Each year, I hear stories from heartbroken parents and see shattered lives because of decisions that were made online. I see the impact of all sorts of digital miscues, small and large. Besides the tragic circumstances that arise, there are also less obvious consequences of failure to navigate a digital world successfully. Who is helping kids figure this stuff out?

One teacher commented that parents should be doing more to monitor and support their own children. I don't disagree with this. I think parents can do more to be aware and help meet these challenges. That's why we've hosted parent workshops and provided information in our newsletters to help parents in this area.

But what I don't agree with is the idea that it's completely the parent's job to address these issues. Our school does not exist in a vacuum. We MUST address the relevant issues of our time and partner with parents to help students be successful. Our school motto is *Learning for Life*. That points to the need for learning that really matters, that will help students be successful, not just on a test, but in living a healthy, balanced, fulfilling life.

In our school, every student must have a device for learning. They can use a school issued Chromebook or they can bring their own device. But using a device is not optional.

This ratchets up our level of responsibility. It's important no matter what. But when our school is so digitally infused, we must work to educate our students about the challenges they face. And we must educate them about the opportunities that technology provides, too.

We are so focused on our curriculum and meeting standards that I think we can forget to pay attention to our students and their needs. We aren't thinking deeply about what is most useful to them now and in the future. We see them as just students. It's all about academics. We are completely focused on making sure they are learning science, history, math, literature, etc. Are they college and career ready? Did they pass the state assessment?

And the one overarching question, the elephant in the room—are you teaching content or are you teaching kids? Because there's a difference. The best teachers are always ready to teach the life-changing lesson. They understand that's the stuff that really makes a lasting impact. Students will forget the foreign language they took in HS, they probably won't ever use the quadratic formula in real life, and reading Victorian literature isn't likely to spark a passion.

I hope you get my point.

We can't afford to not make time for Digital Citizenship or just plain citizenship.

Tech Geek or Teaching Geek?

I think it was during a Twitter chat I first made the comment that you don't have to be a tech geek to use technology effectively to support learning in your classroom. I later polished the wording a bit and asserted that "Classrooms don't need tech geeks who can teach, we need teaching geeks who can use tech."

The message seemed to resonate with educators. But I also received some push back. What's wrong with being a tech-geek? Can we not aim for both? In the end, are the results any different? It seems there is plenty to discuss regarding approaches of using technology to support learning. Let me clarify the thinking behind the quote.

Why teaching geeks?

1. It's more important to get the instructional design right and develop engaging, highly effective learning experiences, with or without tech. Unless the central aim of your curriculum is technology, the tech should support the learning and not the other way around. It's not good practice to find a nifty tech tool and then contrive some way to get it into your lesson, just to wow or impress. That would be akin to using technology like a cool party trick. Not exactly the professional practice that will develop consistent and quality learning for students.

2. Teaching geeks are concerned with more than technology. A teaching geek will do everything possible to increase learning and help all students be successful. They love to learn about teaching, talk about teaching, join with other passionate educators on Twitter, and just be geeky about all things related to their profession. Most of all, they are passionate about student learning. I love to attend EdCamps because the teaching geeks are drawn to these events. Geeks go to Comic-Con. Tech geeks go to CES. Teaching geeks go to Ed-Camps!

3. You don't have to be a technology genius to use tech in the classroom. Many teachers think they can't use technology to support learning because it's not a strength for them. But even if it's not a strength, every teacher can take small steps to utilize technology for learning. Pick just one digital tool that has the potential to enhance your lessons and learn more about it. Our school is in the first year of 1:1 with Chromebooks, so a tool that nearly all our teachers wanted to learn is Google Classroom. It was a good place to start because it serves as a hub for classroom stuff and allows for increased sharing and collaboration.

4. Don't wait, start somewhere. For teachers who lack confidence in technology, it's easy to avoid taking steps to learn new ways to use technology. And this is exactly what we don't want our students to do, to shrink back in the face of something that doesn't come easily. I'm very proud of teachers in our building who have stepped out of their comfort zone to learn new methods with

technology even though it's not their strongest area. It models the type of growth mindset we want to encourage in students.

5. Turn the technology over to your students. Even if you don't know all the ins and outs of using technology, many of your students do. If you give students choice about how to use technology to support their learning, you can incorporate tech even though you aren't the source of all the tech knowledge. It's actually a great thing when students and teachers can learn from each other.

6. So you're a tech geek? That's great. It can be very beneficial to your teaching if you couple your knowledge of technology with an array of other tools that are important to effectiveness in the classroom. How do you build relationships, set expectations, empower learning, and support diverse needs? There are so many factors that contribute to an effective classroom. Technology alone won't result in an excellent classroom experience. But if you can leverage your knowledge of technology to support all the other components of an outstanding classroom, you're a top draft pick for sure!

7. If you are one of the distinguished educators who are both tech geek and teaching geek, you have an obligation to share your knowledge with others. We all want to learn from you.

Is It Time to Move Past Tech Integration?

What is your school's mindset surrounding technology use in the classroom? If you're like a lot of educators, you are probably working to integrate technology into instruction. You might even be discussing the merits of blended learning. But what does it mean to integrate technology? And what is blended learning?

I think those terms are used similarly and seem to indicate a desire for technology to be used more effectively in schools. A common definition of "blended learning" is an education method in which a student learns in part through the delivery of content and instruction via digital and online media with some element of student control over time, place, path, or pace. The increased student agency is the most important part of the entire definition to me.

And yet, I think many schools claim to have blended learning while maintaining a teacher-directed approach. The part about giving some element of student control gets lost in the shuffle as teachers use a variety of 'cool' tools to add pizzazz to the same old lessons they taught before.

Most teachers feel like they need to use technology in their classroom. They are aware of the "technology push" in schools. Everyone seems to be calling for more technology in schools. In fact, spending on K-12 education technology is nearly $10 billion a year. That's a significant push! But to what aim?

Most teachers (but not all) have come around to the idea that it's important to use technology in the classroom. However, far too many think using a PowerPoint and a projector equates to being a forward thinking teacher. But if you change the technology yet don't change your lessons, nothing really changes. It's not enough to take the same old curriculum and methods and just make them digital. Paper and pencil would work just as well for that type of learning.

If you ask teachers why technology is important, you will hear a variety of responses. But one common response I hear is that kids are interested in technology, so using technology will help make kids more interested in learning.

There is an element of truth to this. Some kids do seem to prefer learning that involves digital opportunities. Technology can support student engagement. But it can also support student empowerment. And there's a distinct difference.

A student who is engaged wants to learn something because it's exciting or interesting to them. But a student who is empowered wants to learn something because they find inherent value in the learning for themselves and others. They are choosing to learn because they find meaning in what they are doing. It is more than a fun activity; it's an important pursuit. When we use technology to shift agency to the learner, it is transformational.

We are pushing quickly toward 6 billion smartphones worldwide. We all know smartphones continue to get more powerful each year. In fact, we are using the worst technology right now that we will ever use in our lifetime. Obvious, right? But who knows what might be possible in the near future?

A connected device already gives its owner access to the sum of human knowledge at his or her fingertips.

If your students aren't empowered learners, how will they use this access to reach higher and go further in a world that is rapidly changing? Technology should not be an add-on to learning in the classroom. It shouldn't even be an extension of learning. It's just how we learn in a modern world. One way. Not the only way. But one very important way.

Once, in a presentation, George Couros (@gcouros) remarked, "If I told you the library in your school is just an extra, and I am going to remove it from your school, you would be outraged. Your community would be outraged. You would never allow that. Technology is just as essential to learning as your school library."

I enjoy gardening. This year I'm trying to raise my game and make my garden the best it's ever been. So, I worked extra hard to prepare my soil, select my plants, and find out what works for great gardeners. I talked to friends who are good gardeners, and I regularly conducted research online to answer questions that arose.

And check this out: I am cutting-edge here... I am integrating a shovel, a hoe, and a water hose into my gardening. I went to a garden conference, learned about some cool tools, and have now decided to integrate these tools into my garden plans. What the heck, you say?!? You would never say that you're going to integrate essential tools like a shovel, a hoe, or a water hose into gardening. They're essential. You just use them.

As I used technology to research my garden, I watched YouTube videos and read various blogs and articles to learn more. And it's funny, never once did I think, "I'm now going to integrate some technology into my garden project." I viewed the technology as a helpful tool, a very powerful tool, a potentially transformational tool, to help me be a better gardener. In the same way that my shovel, hoe, and water hose are essential tools for gardening, technology is an essential tool to almost every kind of learning.

At the typical edtech conference, there are a lot of sessions on the *what* and *how* of using tech tools in the classroom. Others share the latest version of a cool app, game, or platform. But I contend that we must always start with *why*. We must understand why we are using technology in the class and have a clear vision of empowering students as adaptable learners. They will need these skills in a world where there will soon be 6 billion smartphone users.

Tech Becomes Invisible

I just ran around our house and did a quick audit. Drum roll, please. I counted 29 web connected devices in our home. We need to have a garage sale. Of course, who would buy a Palm Pre-smartphone? It was a great device in 2010. It just shows how irrelevant a device can be in just a few years. The Palm brand has gone the way of the dinosaurs. Extinct.

Every student at Bolivar High School has a Chromebook to use for learning every day. One of the reasons our school made this move was because we all use technology in our everyday lives, so why should school be any different?

Before 1:1 came to Bolivar High School, using technology was not necessarily an everyday thing. We had computers in the library, in computer labs, a few scattered around in different classrooms, etc. But there was not consistent access. Some students rarely used a device for learning.

As we made the transition to 1:1, we knew every teacher was in a different place in terms of their comfort and skill with using technology. Of course, we are always striving to increase the comfort and knowledge of our staff. And we like to nudge people out of their comfort zone, too.

But since everyone was in a different place, we didn't set any universal expectations. There weren't any quotas or mandates on how to use the Chromebooks. Every teacher is unique, and the curriculum they teach is unique too. So we didn't expect everyone to use the Chromebooks in the same way, or equally as often.

We simply asked everyone to look for ways the technology could provide value and enhance learning for students. And I believe every single teacher in our building used the Chromebooks to support learning in one way or another. That's a good thing.

But even though all our teachers were open-minded and supported the need to go digital as a school, some just didn't see the relevance as strongly for their classroom. I'm guessing there were a whole variety of reasons the devices were used or underused in each classroom.

But consider these questions. Do you have multiple devices in your home? Do you rely on a device daily? Is your ability to connect important to your learning? Do you feel your ability to connect is empowering to you? If you are a digital learner, I'm guessing you answered yes to those questions.

Even if you didn't answer yes to all the previous questions, consider the following. Do most professionals use devices every day? Are the most successful people connected learners? Is our world becoming increasingly digital? Will more opportunities come to those who are competent digital learners?

It's obvious that our students will need to be digital learners to be successful in the future. Heck, they need to be digital learners now to get the most from their school experience. There are tools and resources available online that far exceed the resources we could provide otherwise.

And almost every school has realized this to some extent. I haven't visited a school yet that isn't using computers or digital learning in some way.

But technology should be an everyday thing. It shouldn't be a special event, a remediation strategy, a canned learning program, or an enrichment activity after the real learning is done. It should be an authentic part of learning. It should empower us, connect us, and give us new opportunities. It should stimulate curiosity, creativity, and help us solve problems. When it is used regularly it almost becomes invisible. It becomes more about learning and less about technology.

Technology can be used to support learning, but it can also be used in ways that transform learning. It is far more likely to be transformational when it is used regularly. It just becomes a normal part of learning and not an add-on or special event.

Now you might be thinking that using technology in every class, every day sounds rigid. And don't we sometimes need a break from tech? Don't we need to unplug occasionally? Aren't students using technology every day anyway? Some students are probably using technology too much, right?

We absolutely need to keep some balance in mind. Too much screen time can be bad for us. We need to unplug from time to time. I once took a month-long break. There are benefits to pausing and stepping away from devices.

But that's not a reason for limiting tech in the classroom when it could be so helpful. I recently learned about the Project Red research study, a large-scale look at practices in 997 schools across the U.S. The report includes seven key findings about the effective use of technology in schools.[1]

One of the key findings showed that schools must incorporate technology into daily teaching to realize the benefits. The daily use of tech in core classes correlates highly to these education success measures (ESMs): better discipline, better attendance, and increased college attendance.

The Project Red report shows how powerful technology can be when it is used effectively. There were all sorts of positive outcomes in schools that implemented technology well, including the benefits found from the daily use of technology instead of intermittent use.

Leverage

Using technology as a consistent practice is helpful to learning, but we must use it in ways to leverage skills and transform learning. If we want adaptable, self-directed learners, students need opportunities to use technology in ways that allow them to connect, create, and share.

1. Authentic Audience

It's sad that most work students do in school ultimately ends up in a trash can. The audience for their efforts is usually the teacher and maybe their classmates, but rarely is work shared beyond the school walls. By using digital tools, it is possible to share work to a potentially unlimited audience, and it's possible to curate the work so it's available forever. Say goodbye to the trash can finish.

When students work for an authentic audience, it is potentially a game changer. Instead of just completing assignments in a manner that is "good enough" they now want the work to be just plain "good." And how the work is received can provide excellent feedback. An authentic audience multiplies the possibilities for feedback. As any blogger can attest, having an audience changes everything, and really makes you think about your ideas.

2. Creativity

While using technology is not necessary to be creative, access can facilitate many new ways to express ideas in original ways. Digital content is easily captured, shared, and combined as an outlet to creative thought. In short, digital tools give rise to more possibilities for creation and innovation.

3. 24/7 Learning

Access to a connected device makes it possible for learning to continue beyond the classroom. Sure, I guess that sort of happened before. You took your textbook home to study, right? Well, some people did. But now learners have the sum of human knowledge available on their smartphone, anytime, anywhere. When I need to learn just about anything, one of my top sources is YouTube. It's helped me repair our vacuum and help the kids with algebra homework. It's a shame it's blocked in so many schools.

4. Global Connections

We learn so much more when we connect and share with others. Now we can connect with anyone in the world with minimal effort. It's possible to learn directly from experts in the field. Classrooms can connect across oceans. Global connections allow us to see diverse perspectives and understand problems with implications beyond the local community.

5. Learner Agency

Technology provides opportunities for individual learning paths. Not everyone has to learn in the same time, in the same space, with the same lessons. Students can learn about things that are important to them, in ways that they choose. Technology allows for students to take greater ownership and be more self-directed. Learning is more meaningful when it is personal.

6. Collaboration and Communication

Technology is transformational when it allows learners to work in teams, share ideas, and collaborate on new projects. Learners can work together and share ideas even when they are apart. Digital tools allow for amazing new ways to connect around sharing ideas and tasks.

7. Curiosity and Inquiry

Technology allows students to pursue answers to their own questions. True understanding doesn't happen by memorizing facts or seeking right answers. Understanding is developed by developing questions, interpreting information, and drawing conclusions. Curiosity taps into a sense of wonder and makes learning come alive. Technology provides access to information and inspiration to magnify curiosity and inquiry.

System Failure

Some people blame technology for a lack of thinking skills in today's generation. Of course, that line of thinking is typical isn't it? We tend to think we're so much smarter than the generation before us and much wiser than the generation after us. Instead of valuing how we may think differently than others, we only see the difference as a failure on their part.

But there are some who think technology is harmful to thinking and learning. I've been asked if we are relying too much on technology. Are kids able to think for themselves? What happens if they don't have access to the technology? Will they know what to do then? Sure, they can look up information they need, but what if they don't have the internet at their fingertips?

I don't think we lose our ability to think because we have access technology. Just because I can find information doesn't mean that good thinking isn't required to make sense of it. Sure, technology makes some tasks easier, so maybe we don't have to think as much in those areas. But there is plenty of thinking that technology can't do. Google doesn't have answers. It has information. We find answers through how we make meaning of information. People develop answers to the truly interesting questions.

So what happens if you don't have access to technology? What happens when the power goes out in your house? What happens when you run out of gas in your car? What happens when my 26HP zero-turn radius 60-inch deck mower breaks down? Well, I get it fixed. I'm not going back to mowing 3-acres with a scythe like 100 years ago.

Digital Leadership

Digital learning will continue to play an increasing role in classrooms. Will computers replace teachers? I don't think so. As long as relationships matter in learning, I believe teachers will be irreplaceable. But teachers will need to become more skilled at using digital tools for learning and helping students become stronger digital learners. Students who can leverage their skills with technology will have a tremendous advantage in life over those who will not embrace these opportunities.

As technology plays an increasing role in life and learning, we need educators to be digital leaders. We need to develop our own skills and constantly be learning about technology opportunities. We need to model the productive and positive uses of technology. And we need to encourage students to use tech to create, connect, and share. Digital leadership isn't just for administrators. Every person who is important in the life of a child should help to shape these skills. Teachers have an important role to play. Effective leadership today, in the school and in the classroom, must involve effective digital leadership. And that will only be truer in the future.

CHAPTER 13

Embrace Change

In the 1960 Democratic Primary Elections, John F Kennedy utilized television to his incredible advantage. But Johnson, even though he badly wanted the nomination, was hesitant to enter the race largely because he feared defeat. He wanted it almost too badly, and would not publicly announce as a candidate. His fear of losing and fear of being humiliated in defeat paralyzed him until at the last moment, he declared. But it was too late.

While Johnson had been reluctant to take a risk, Kennedy was developing a highly effective campaign machine. He traveled the nation building support, but even more importantly, he leveraged the power of television to his great advantage. Every chance he got, he was in front of the American public, in their living rooms, connecting with them through their television sets.

Johnson thought television was a waste of time. He thought Kennedy was too flashy and that he lacked substance. Johnson was proud of his accomplishments as a leader in the Senate. He blasted Kennedy for his weak record as a senator, noting that JFK had accomplished very little as a lawmaker. Kennedy rarely even showed up for work. He was too busy running a campaign for President.

Regardless of his Senate record, JFK won the nomination. In a strange twist, he invited LBJ onto his ticket as his vice president. Begrudgingly, Johnson accepted the offer to be Kennedy's running mate. Kennedy went on to win the election in 1960, beating Republican Richard Nixon.

In the same way, Johnson failed to recognize the power of television, too many educators today are not adapting to the digital transformation of the modern age, a revolution even more powerful than television. They are struggling to adapt to these new literacies. They think of social media and other digital tools as optional at best, and at worst they completely reject that these tools have any merit for learners.

Some pay lip service to the idea that technology is important, but they do very little to model the use of digital tools, in their own lives or in their classrooms. They rarely use technology for learning, and when they do it is such a special event that it is more of a gimmick than a way of doing business. They cling to their content as if it must be the most important thing for their students to know, without ever questioning how irrelevant it might be for some.

Do reading, writing, and math skills still matter? Absolutely. Every person should have skills in these traditional literacies, but we can't stop there. Those skills are just the beginning. Students need to also know how to apply these basic skills in ways that generate value in today's world. They need to practice these skills in modern applications. Learning digital literacies is not about learning gadgets or gimmicks. It's about learning how to collaborate, communicate, create, and think in a connected, information-rich world.

So instead of writing that research paper, ask students to create blogs. Incorporate social media into studies of literature and history. Reach out to experts in various fields to demonstrate the power of connections. Examine how modern films, music, and art impact the world of science and social science. Develop a classroom culture that goes beyond memorizing and testing. We need students to develop the skills of makers, designers, and innovators.

If we are slow to respond to how our world is changing, we are doing our students a disservice. We can't afford to make our own comfort and preferences the priority, now when seismic shifts are happening all around us that demand we change. If we want our students to win at life in a digital world, we must act as if it's that important. Our students are counting on us. We must lead.

If educators fail to adapt to the rapidly changing world, our students will suffer. Someone else will get the job. Someone else will solve the problem. Or even worse, the problem won't get solved. We will limit the possibilities of our most important resource, our children, simply because we didn't take a risk, try something new, or continue to be a learner. Like LBJ, if we are slow to adapt, it will result in failure. We all stand to lose.

Nothing Changes

Nothing's gonna change if nothing changes.

If we want to change student learning for the better, we must be willing to change teaching.

You may not like the changes. You may think technology plays too large a role. That life is too complex today. That social media is denigrating social skills. You may long for a simpler time. But that's not helpful to moving forward. Progress can be hard.

There are two things most people complain about:

   1. The way things are.

   2. Change.

Our progress is sometimes both a blessing and a burden. We gain something but often at a cost. Our work is to help create better thinkers. We want to see students who can lead progress in a positive direction. We don't want change for the sake of change. We want to see people's lives improved. We want to improve the human condition.

Rock Solid Truth

Are you *old school*? You've probably heard educators described that way before.

"He doesn't allow students to have cell phones in his class. He's *old school!*"

I'm guessing I haven't been described as *old school*. I like pushing forward into uncharted territory too much. I enjoy trying new things in our school and doing things in ways that challenge the status quo. But in a way, I think I'm old school.

That's because I believe some things are forever true. There are fundamentals of teaching and learning that are universal and unchanging. There are core principles that we can always count on. There are foundations of learning that stand the test of time. And we should never abandon the essential truths of learning for something shiny and new. We should always move forward and build on these truths, but we should never abandon them.

Smashing Watermelons

When he wasn't smashing watermelons, prop comedian Gallagher had a bit with a time capsule. He would make fun of some object or invention of modern life (from the 70s or 80s) and then put it in the time capsule. He would then proclaim, "This is how we show the people in the future how dumb we were back here in the past."

8-track tapes, soap on a rope, bell bottoms, pet rocks, and candy cigarettes. How is that for dumb? Who would think it's a good idea to give kids sugar to help them fantasize about smoking? The Ethel Merman Disco Album. Yeah, that's actually a thing. Might be the worst thing ever.

None of these examples had lasting significance. They were just a fad. But some things transcend time. Not material things, but ideas. Truth, goodness, and beauty. Liberty, justice, and equality. These ideas transcend. They are time machine worthy. They reveal the past and propel us into the future.

But other things are just a moment in time. They have their moment and then they fade into memory. They are worthy of the time capsule but nothing more.

Perfecting the Past

We cannot just try to get better at the stuff we've always done. Sure, some things will always be relevant. Our basic human needs haven't changed much. But how we meet those needs, the methods of our learning, our tools, our social structures are all changing quickly. Ray McNulty (@Ray_McNulty) warns us not to try to perfect the past. We need to make decisions about what we need to keep doing, stop doing, and start doing.

We've been doing a lot of the same things in education. The system has looked much the same for generations. It's time to do some new things. But it will be built on what we've done before. It will be built on the ideas from the past. It will be built on what we know works.

But out of the lessons of the past, we must step boldly forward into the future. We must embrace change, seek new ideas, and allow creativity to flow into our concept of school. We need to create learning opportunities that prepare students for the world they will live in. It's not the same world we grew up in.

9 Reasons Educators Should Embrace Change

In his book, *The Innovator's Mindset*, George Couros goes in-depth explaining the how and why of innovation in education. He makes a compelling case for the power of innovation to improve schools. As I've learned from Couros, it's possible for every educator to be an innovator.[1]

Innovation requires a willingness to look at problems with new eyes and to see challenges as opportunities. Students are going to need skills for their future beyond the academic achievement goals that have been the overwhelming focus of the past. To help students be future ready, schools will need to help students become adaptable learners.

Schools need to help students develop leadership skills. They must be global citizens and understand how to work with people from different cultures and backgrounds. They need to solve complex problems, work in teams, communicate effectively, and have digital skills. We need to make creativity a top priority. But the only way schools will meet the demands of the changing world around us is to innovate and embrace change.

If you still aren't convinced, here are nine reasons educators should embrace change.

1. Change is inevitable. It isn't productive to resist it because it is impossible to avoid. Change will happen. When you embrace it, you can influence the direction and outcomes of the change. Change either happens to you, or you take ownership of it. Most of us become comfortable with things the way they are, even though everything around us may be changing. The only way we can provide schooling that is relevant is to accept change and learn and grow.

2. You can make a difference. Some people resist change because they believe it won't matter anyway. But your efforts to embrace change will create better learning opportunities for students. Believe in your ability to use change to make a positive impact.

3. Growth means risk. You can't grow without risking something. We stay with what's familiar because we are comfortable with it, but that's not progress. We need to have a growth mindset. When we take this approach, we thrive on taking risks and trying things that aren't a sure thing. We want to take risks. When we fail, it's not fatal. It's just proof we are trying.

4. You can't expect to do the same thing and get different results. Most every teacher is not entirely satisfied with how students are learning. Most see problems with student motivation or engagement. Is it reasonable to think these issues will improve without changing teaching or education? Change and innovation are necessary to solve the problems we see in our schools.

5. Giving up "good" can help you find "great." As Jim Collins pointed out, good is the enemy of great. It is hard to embrace change when things are going well. My test scores are good. I'm a respected teacher. Our school is a shining star in our community. When things are going well, it's harder to see the need for change. But we should never be satisfied. We should always seek ways to improve learning for our students.

6. New opportunities are waiting. Letting go is hard. It can be very difficult to put aside the things that we find most comfortable. But when you step out of your comfort zone, there is potential for incredible fulfillment and reward. We stand to gain so much for our students and for our own personal fulfillment. Innovation and change start with a belief that there might be a better way. We have to believe these opportunities await.

7. Personal preferences can be harmful. Some people resist change because of their personal preferences. Even if they see an idea has the potential to improve things for students and learning, they may not embrace it because it makes

them uncomfortable. It's not what they prefer. Educators cannot afford this mindset. You must be flexible in your state of mind and welcome any opportunity that can move education forward.

8. Your students need to see adaptability. You can model change and innovation for your students. When you are innovative in the classroom, students are more likely to become adaptable, innovative learners. These skills will serve them well. We can't expect students to be innovative unless educators are first willing to be innovative.

9. Leaders embrace change. Effective leaders embrace change and help others embrace change too. Whether you have a formal leadership position or not, your school needs leaders who are problem solvers and who are willing to try new things. Every person can be a leader. Your words and actions can help positive change occur in your school.

> *Twenty years from now, you will be more disappointed by the things that you didn't do than by the ones you did do. Dare. Dream. Discover. —Mark Twain*

Be Willing to Change Your Mind

If you can't change your mind, you can't change anything. Smart people change their minds. They don't hold onto their beliefs. They change over time.

Be willing to subject even your most favored beliefs to scrutiny. Be open to new information and check your assumptions regularly.

When an idea or belief doesn't work out in practice.

When you have outgrown an idea or belief.

When the world changes and makes an idea or belief obsolete.

Move the Needle

Some things are beyond our ability to change. Sometimes I feel like I'm not anywhere close to affecting the kind of change I would like to see. But I remind myself to do what I can. It's important to meet people where they are, to understand and honor the culture as it is, but to also try to move it forward. I want to make a difference. I want to stand out just enough to make people uncomfortable. It's the only way to make things better. We must be real and see the future through the time machine. We must move. We must search for a better way and be willing to step out of our comfort zone. It's a choice.

Dear Defender of Status Quo

Dear Defender of the Status Quo,

The status quo does not need your help.

It is a powerful force on its own. It has inertia on its side. And fear. And control.

You feel safer with what's familiar, but you're not.

In the end, failure to change makes you antique, obsolescent, irrelevant, and eventually extinct.

You can see that the world is changing around you. Fast. Really fast. The evidence is everywhere. But what are you doing about it?

The status quo won't prepare students for the challenges they will face. Change is inevitable, and you are needed as a change-maker.

Is your teaching today much different from how you were taught? Are your lessons preparing students for yesterday or tomorrow?

Desks are lined in straight rows. Students listen for instructions. Complete Assignments. Take tests. How is the experience unique to the world today and not the world of 50 years ago?

You are more than a curriculum implementer. You are a positive change maker.

You work with the most valuable resource in the world—children.

You matter.

A lot has been pushed on you I know. Your work has been devalued, disrespected, and run down.

Your work is more than a test score.

But it won't help to circle the wagons and just hang on to the old.

It's tempting to become cynical. To resent the bureaucrats or pundits who want to change you from the outside. Who want to create a marketplace for a child's education.

Keep the focus on your students.

Keep an eye on tomorrow.

Don't let your school become a time capsule.

Be a champion for change. Don't wait for it to happen to you. Drive the change from your platform. You have a voice.

You are a leader.

People want to know what you stand for, not just what you stand against. I want to know.

Share your story.

Inspire.

You can let the challenges cause you to clench your fists and hang on to what you know, or you can reach for something new and be the one who creates a better tomorrow for public schools, and ultimately for kids.

Dream.

If technology isn't your strength, that's okay. But how are you growing? How are you becoming a stronger digital learner?

Grow.

You lead by example. Your example is your greatest opportunity for influence. Your students are watching.

Don't allow change to be something done to you. Be empowered.

Your work can't be replaced by a machine, but only if you connect and relate and stay relevant. You may be a kid's best chance. You can be a game-changer.

Spread hope.

Remember to always teach kids first, and then curriculum. Teach them how to think. How to work the problem. How to adapt to whatever they might face.

Create excitement around learning. Make it count for something besides a grade or a diploma or a test score.

The status quo is a taker. It takes your passion, your zest, your difference. It tries to make you like everyone else.

Stand out.

You are not an interchangeable part and neither are your students. Make your classroom more artwork and less assembly line.

And please, please don't be a defender of the status quo...

Sincerely,

The Future Driven Educator

CHAPTER 14

Making Learning Meaningful

W hy have we placed such a high value on sense-making over meaning-making? Sense-making involves understanding and demonstrating a content or skill. Much of the work we do in school is related to sense-making and there is nothing inherently wrong with this. We need to know facts and learn skills. But why don't we make greater efforts to connect sense-making with things that bring meaning? Meaning is what helps us to really make sense of the world. It's coming to a place where we understand why our sense-making matters. Meaning gives relevance to our learning.

Daniel Pink explains in his book *Drive* that people are more effective, more motivated, and more connected to their work, and all areas of life when conditions exist that allow for autonomy, mastery, and purpose. When we have autonomy, we feel we have a voice and a choice. When we can do things well (mastery), it makes us want to try even harder and do even more. And when we have a sense of purpose, we feel our contributions matter and that what we contribute is bigger than ourselves.[1]

These conditions are far more powerful than extrinsic rewards because deep down we know that things that are most meaningful are ones that stand the test of time. Extrinsic rewards satisfy for a moment, but they don't deeply satisfy. They only feed appetites for more recognition, more rewards, or more pleasures. We need meaning, not more stuff, not better grades, not more rules or policies.

In our hurried, success-driven, hyper-connected culture, there is a hunger for meaning in ways like never before. We need something greater than ourselves and our shallow appetites (more stuff, more fame, more instant gratification).

So how does this all translate to the classroom? Let's ask students to do stuff that really matters, to themselves and to others. Learning shouldn't happen in isolation from real impact. Open the world and find ways for students to make a difference now. Give students the freedom and flexibility to do something amazing. As I think about the learning experiences from my school days that I remember the most, they are ones that were personally meaningful to me. We can't expect sense-making to last beyond the test if we don't help students have a personal meaning connected to the learning.

Make learning personally meaningful and students will find their passions and become self-determined, lifelong learners.

I Love My Job

I was eager to get home after a long day, but the checkouts were backed up. I randomly picked a line since they were all busy. But this time I picked the right one. Before I knew it I was on my way home. The clerk in the line I picked was giving such a great effort that I noticed.

When it was almost my turn to check out, I applauded the clerk's service to the customer in front of me, "Wow, she really knows how to make a line disappear." The customer smiled and agreed. I added, "She's really a hard worker."

The clerk then replied with these magical words, "I love my job." She proceeded to double bag all my cold items, rush around to help load bags of groceries into my cart, and even made a suggestion about a type of potato chips she liked that were similar to the ones I bought.

On my way home, I called Walmart and asked for the store manager, explaining that I had just received amazing service and wanted to commend the employee for her outstanding job. The store manager was not available, but I did talk with a shift manager and shared my story, referring to the employee personally since I took note of her name badge. The manager was very appreciative of the phone call and said she would share the compliment in their store meeting.

Isn't it great when people go above and beyond for a job well-done? We all appreciate having excellent service provided, whether it is in the drive-thru, the doctor's office, or the checkout line.

Each of us gets to choose our attitude about our work each day. I once knew someone who worked as a checkout clerk at Walmart and complained nonstop about her job. Each time I would see her at her station she barely moved a muscle, wore a frown, and said almost nothing to any of the customers. Her attitude was a choice, just like the clerk who chose to share with me, "I love my job."

Everyone matters. Every job matters. And I am thankful I was taught to respect hard work and to respect people regardless of their level of education, how much money they have, or what kind of job they do.

Even though every job matters, I think our work as educators is especially meaningful. We work with children every day, and we have the opportunity to help shape their future. Every word and every deed makes an impact and can be used to build up or tear down a child's dreams.

Since our work is so significant in the life of a child, we owe it to him or her and to her parents, to be our very best every day. We must be all in 100% or we are doing a disservice to our profession and to the future of a child.

So what kind of teacher do you want for your child? I bet you want one who goes above and beyond to do a great job every day, even when it's not easy.

Learning for Life

Education without values, as useful as it is, seems rather to make man a more clever devil. —C.S. Lewis

If your students are proficient, do you have a successful school? Do test scores determine the level of victory in your classroom? Where do you get your sense of meaning and purpose as an educator?

The problem with success is it usually involves comparison with others. How do I measure up? Did I win? Was I the best? Was I the smartest? When individuals, teams, or schools are focused on success, anything less than first place is disappointing. Setbacks and failures can be devastating.

We should aim for excellence.

Excellence is a habit of mind. It's about being the best we can be. Excellence is giving your best effort, maximizing your talents and gifts, and reaching for your highest potential. When you seek excellence, you realize failures and successes are inevitable along the way. Excellence is about doing things that matter, that lift up others, and that make a positive difference in the world.

Even when you seek success, you may still find failure. But when you seek excellence, success usually finds you. Don't hang your value on whether you win or not. Strive to be the very best you can be. Strive to learn, grow, and stretch yourself. If you do that, the wins will usually come.

Teaching standards without inspiring passion, hope, or empathy might still result in success. You might get the high scores on the test. But that's not excellence. Your commitment to getting better needs to be more important than your commitment to getting better scores.

Learning should be meaningful. It's not about proficiency or a test score. It's about making a difference and cultivating value. How can I be more valuable to my community? How can I learn things that help me become a better person?

We teach our students well so they can help themselves, others, and society. We want them to strive for excellence.

When learning is meaningful, it leads to passion. Passion leads to perseverance. It leads to a life well lived.

If students graduate with a diploma, but without a sense of mission or purpose we are falling short in our mission and purpose. Education is bigger than the standards we have to teach. Education is learning more about who you are and how you contribute to making the world a better place.

Future Stories

For decades, teacher Bruce Farrer has given his students an assignment to write letters to their future selves. He saves each of one the letters, carefully organizing them, and after 20 years he tracks down each student's address and mails the letter back. The detective work required in locating each student is significant. But the impact of his project is immense. The stories are heartwarming and sincere, even life changing. Imagine the power of reading a letter from yourself 20 years removed from the current you. The shift in perspective might seem startling and profound.

But what a wonderful assignment. It transcends the short-lived value of most assignments. What do our students have to show for their years of school work? How often does an assignment is school have value beyond learning a standard or getting a grade? I think it should happen all the time.

But this assignment is powerful at more than one moment in time. It's time machine teaching at its best. It transcends time. When students wrote the letters as high school students, it forced them to think about the future. 20 years seems like an eternity at that time in your life. It seems like you will never see the day you receive this letter from yourself. But it forces the writer to think about another time, a future time, a future world. It forces consideration of who I am, what I want from life, and how my story will unfold.

A YouTube video documents Bruce Farrer and his letters to our future selves.[2]

A Trebuchet and a Video Game

I asked my sons, Drew and Cooper, about what was the most meaningful learning experience they had in high school. They are both college students now. They didn't even hesitate in recollecting.

Drew was on a project team in physics class assigned the task of building a trebuchet, or catapult. The team was responsible for planning the design, gathering the materials, and ultimately building a machine that would launch an object further than any of the other teams in their class.

I remember them working on this in our basement. They had great discussions as they made decisions about their strategy. I also remember the day of the competition. In the practice rounds, their trebuchet was middle of the pack. But when it counted, they launched the winning distance. And it wasn't even close.

Their initial looks of surprise and astonishment gave way to excited celebration. They were thrilled to win the contest. It was a moment they won't ever forget.

My youngest son Cooper has always been passionate about video games. So, when he had the opportunity to sign-up for an FBLA (Future Business Leaders of America) contest to design a game he was all in. But he soon learned this was going to be very challenging. He spent hours upon hours teaching himself the game design platform he used. I remember being very nervous he wasn't going to meet the deadline for it to be finished, but he did.

He and his friend Noah worked up their presentation to pitch the game. We were thrilled when we learned they advanced to the national level. They would present in Nashville over the summer. Lori and I were in the audience when they presented at nationals. Wow, I was blown away. They did a great job.

But I never expected what happened later at the awards ceremony. After all, there are thousands of bright kids here competing, right? But when the winners were announced, Cooper and Noah took 2nd in the nation. It was thrilling!

So, what is similar about these learning experiences that were so meaningful for Drew and Cooper?

It was a project.

There was teamwork.

There was a mentor (teacher).

There was risk of failure and celebration of success.

These were learning experiences and not just lessons. They had to rely on their thinking, teach themselves, make critical decisions that would lead to success or failure, and work with others toward a common goal. These experiences may not have been most efficient for covering standards, but they were far more valuable than learning content and taking an exam.

Solving for X

What types of problems are you asking your students to solve? Are they problems on a sheet of paper or are they real problems with real consequences?

What if your classroom or school was devoted to finding a cure for cancer? Is it possible for kids to discover such a thing? I don't know. But how many lives has cancer touched? Would kids be motivated to learn and make a difference if they thought they could contribute to such an important cause?

There isn't a shortage of real problems in our world that need someone's time and attention. There are problems that need a different approach. There are problems the experts haven't solved or that have been largely ignored. Wouldn't it be great if students were coming to school to help solve these problems?

Why shouldn't kids be making important contributions right now? We have unbelievable power in our schools if we just tap into the collective genius that is walking the halls.

Alan November observed, "Today, very little of the work we give students in school provides them with the sense that they are making a contribution to anything other than their own educational progress toward graduation."[3]

If we want to give students work that's relevant, give them work that makes a difference. Kids have important contributions to make right now. They can be helping, assisting, making, serving, creating, inventing, encouraging, improving, planning, building, giving, and supporting. They can be doing stuff that matters now and in the future.

---

7 Ways to Make Learning More Meaningful

1. Build Relationships

If learning is going to be meaningful in your classroom, it won't happen without building relationships with students. Get to know your students. And let your students get to know you. Connect with them, invest in them, and care about them. When a teacher is willing to meet a student need, it creates an environment where caring matters.

2. Tell Stories of Triumph and Tragedy

Stories are extremely powerful for conveying meaning. Your personal stories are especially powerful. You may think you don't have extraordinary stories to tell, but that's just not true. We all have stories that would benefit our students. We can also tell the stories of others who have overcome obstacles, who are heroes of the discipline, or who have made an extraordinary impact in the world. Find ways to connect the stories to your content. It just takes a little creativity. It's so easy to find inspiring, hopeful stories on YouTube that you can share too.

3. Serve Others

Find ways to connect what students are learning to service opportunities in your community. Challenge them to do something to give back and then let them share their stories. Your students can do projects that involve learning the curriculum and making a difference in the world. Your students could be creating prosthetic limbs with a 3D printer, they could be creating a more environmentally friendly school, or they could be inventing a backpack that converts to a tent to keep people who are homeless warm. These are actual examples of classrooms serving others and making a difference.

4. Solve Real Problems

There are plenty of problems in every school and community that need solving. We have significant challenges in our nation and worldwide. What if students were not only discussing these problems in their classes but working on possible solutions? Imagine what might happen. Imagine what problems might get solved. But these kids aren't experts. How will they solve these problems? Let's be reminded experts built the Titanic and amateurs built the Ark. Don't ever underestimate what might be possible. We can't put limits on our kids.

5. Champion a Cause

In addition to solving real world problems, your students can support causes that matter to them. Young people are eager to have their voice heard. They want to speak out on issues that are important to them. If we want to develop leaders, we need to provide opportunities for students to lead.

6. Be Passionate

Learning is most meaningful when it is filled with passion. Educators should be the most excited people on the planet about learning and kids. When you bring your passion to the classroom, it helps your students get excited too. When students see how you value learning, they will see learning as meaningful too. One of the reasons that learning lacks meaning is kids haven't found the inspiration for learning. We must be just as concerned about inspiring them as we are about the actual content.

7. Invite Reflection

For students to experience learning as meaningful, we need to provide opportunities for reflection. I realize there is a lot of information to learn, and we feel the press of time. But it is essential to make time to reflect. Opportunity for reflection helps students to consider what parts of the learning were most meaningful, what went well, where did it go wrong, and how can I apply this to a situation in my life. Thinking is always made better through reflection. We have to look back on our learning process and learn from it.

Beyond Ourselves

Most of what we do is a search for significance. Maybe everything. We want to matter. We want to belong. We want to feel accepted, and we want to avoid rejection.

We want our life to count for something beyond what we can see and understand. We want to transcend mediocrity and do something worthwhile and important. We want excellence. We want to be part of something bigger than ourselves.

That's why the idea of time machines is powerful to capture the imagination. Time machines allow us to transcend. They tap into something beyond us. They take us beyond ourselves to another time and place. They break limits.

You've probably experienced things in your life that made you feel you were part of something extraordinary. It might have been a view from a mountain peak, an extraordinary moment, a time you accomplished something far beyond what you thought was possible, the birth of your child, or another miraculous happening.

In these moments, we get a sense of meaning far beyond the ordinary. We feel connected, inspired, hopeful, and filled with life. We need to strive to bring these moments into school. They happen from time to time. They should happen more often. We must think beyond ourselves and make learning meaningful.

CHAPTER 15

Pushing Forward

The real source of wealth and capital in this new era is not material things. It is the human mind, the human spirit, the human imagination, and our faith in the future. —Steve Forbes

I enjoy running. It keeps me sane. Some might say it's not working that great. Anyway, I meet up with some friends most every Sunday morning and we run 8 or 10 miles before church. My kids think that's crazy. They especially think it's crazy that I think it's fun.

Over the years, I've run a couple of marathons. I plan to run another one this fall. There is nothing that has physically tested me to my limits more than the experience of running a marathon. Honestly, each time it was over, I wasn't sure if I'd ever want to do it again. But then I eventually forget how bad I hurt, and I become restless for the challenge again.

There is something in me that stirs and wants to test my limits. There's something that says you can do it better and faster than before. There's something in me that promises to train harder and be more disciplined. There's something that says you'll be better and stronger if you do this.

We are all focused on the future in different ways. We have calendars to plan our lives. We have hopes and dreams that are out there somewhere. It seems we're always thinking, what's next? What race will I run? What mountain will I climb? We look forward in anticipation to what the future holds. But we also dread other things we might face. The unknown can be both exciting and terrifying.

But our future is out there and what we do today will help to shape it. We can avoid the challenges and play it safe. We can worry about the pain, the risks, the chance of loss. Or, we can go forward boldly and challenge ourselves. To reach our potential, we must refuse to accept the limits and always be pushing forward.

No Limits

We limit ourselves. And we allow others to place limits on us. Too often we're locked in the time capsule, allowing the constraints of the past to hold us back. It's important to learn from the past, but you must not stay there. You cannot allow yesterday's wins or losses keep you from the possibilities that are in front of you. You don't have to be stuck in a time capsule. You don't have to accept the limits.

Your classroom doesn't have to be a time capsule.

People will try to put limits on you. The critics are always ready to pounce. People will doubt you. Even recently, I have felt the sting of disapproval from critics. I've felt the pain of feeling misunderstood.

But I'm not upset about my critics. I know I've placed far more limits on myself. When I impose limits on myself, it's not because of critics. I have a choice every day to settle for less and let mediocrity creep in. Or to find another gear and push myself to grow. Peanuts cartoonist Charles Schultz was right when he said, "Life is like a 10-speed bike. Most of us have gears we never use."

There is something in all of us that holds us back. It keeps us from believing in our dreams. It tells us to play it safe and that our big ideas are silly or don't make sense. Abraham Maslow observed, "Life is an ongoing process of choosing between safety (out of fear) and risk (for growth). Make the growth choice a dozen times a day."

So with that in mind: if you had no fear, what would you do? Use that question to push forward.

I am always pushing to never get stuck in the same gear. I don't want to be a relic of the time capsule. I want to continue to grow. I want to be like the time machine. And I want that for you, too. You have amazing abilities, unbelievable creativity, and talents and gifts that are only yours. You can transcend the boundaries that you or others perceive.

As Leonardo da Vinci said, "All great Acts of Genius began with the same consideration: Do not be constrained by your present reality." There will always be naysayers who will say it can't be done. They'll say it's impossible. But if you *bury can't*, you will contribute in ways that are transcendent. The ripples of your work will last. You will make a lasting impact, and you will help to make dreams come true for yourself and your students.

In the book *If It Ain't Broke...Break It!* Robert Kriegel and Louis Patler write, "We don't have a clue as to what people's limits are. All the tests, stopwatches, and finish lines in the world can't measure human potential. When someone is pursuing their dream, they'll go far beyond what seem to be their limitations. The potential that exists within us is limitless and largely untapped."[1]

Be the Difference

We can't settle or get comfortable. Life these days is moving fast. And we must keep moving too. We must keep thinking, trying, iterating, challenging, believing, and creating. Every single one of us has what we need to make a difference for ourselves and for our students.

I believe in you. I believe you can make your school and your life more like a time machine and less like a time capsule. But you must believe in yourself too. You can be an adaptable learner. You can create a brighter future and better tomorrow. You can create change that will prepare your students for an unpredictable world.

In a recent talk at Northpoint Church, Danielle Strickland shared a hopeful message about using what you must make an impact for others. Danielle is an officer in the Salvation Army, and she has worked for many years to serve people in need. She has been especially involved in fighting human trafficking.[2]

She told the story of a woman who wanted to help girls trapped in the most desperate circumstances. This woman lived in a country with legal prostitution, and there was a known brothel in her community. But she felt like there was nothing she could do. She thought, "What could I ever do help these women?" She didn't see any way she could have an impact.

Danielle asked her what she would normally do to help someone in need. What if someone was in an accident? Or someone new moved into your neighborhood?

"I would bake them cupcakes," she replied.

"Okay, do that."

And so, the woman made the cupcakes and showed up at the brothel to deliver them. And that initial visit led to a weekly visit. And those weekly visits led to a new strategy. Now 68 different brothels in 12 different cities, speaking 10 different languages get weekly visits from Salvation Army volunteers, complete with baked goods. It even led to trafficking rings being closed and the opportunity to testify before Parliament.

Cupcakes can change the world! Actually, they can't. Cupcakes are awesome, but what can really change the world is people who are willing to use what they have to help other people. That's what it takes to be the difference. It's people who are willing to bake cupcakes to try to make a difference. It's not waiting until we have it all figured out, but using what we have to offer help.

That's what educators should strive to do each day. When we bring our talents and abilities to bear in the classroom, our students will have better opportunities for learning, and we can help them overcome any obstacles that stand in their way. It won't happen by just going through the motions. We must be willing to invest ourselves and take a risk.

David and Goliath

My parents cared about me, and they cared about my education. They poured themselves into my life and helped me to grow into who I am today. Not every kid has that. My parents believed in me, and I knew it. They helped prepare me. I didn't always listen to their advice, but the lessons they taught would always stick with me.

I remember when I was a little kid we had this recording of a song that told the story of David and Goliath. I remember I would play the record over and over and pretend that I was the David who slew the giant. Actually, I think I played both parts. I would hurl the stone at Goliath and then run over and fall down as it struck him in the head.

Of course, the story of David and Goliath is one of no limits. David was just a little shepherd boy who most thought was poorly equipped to battle a giant Philistine. But David used what he had, and with God's help, he could defeat the enemy.

My parents taught me these lessons from a very early age. I learned to believe in my own possibilities. I learned that with God's help I could do anything.

But many of our students don't have that type of encouragement. So we as educators have the opportunity to fill that gap. We can help them see the possibilities in their lives. A caring educator can make a huge difference in the life of a child. Other than my parents, I don't know of any person that changed the direction of my life more than Coach Radford.

At a time in my life when I had so many doubts about myself, he believed in me. He helped me to believe in my dreams and made me feel like I could do it. He supported and built upon that foundation my parents provided.

Being a future driven educator is doing what's best for students in the long run. It's elevating human potential. It's making things better right now so we can create a better tomorrow. It's breaking boundaries and getting uncomfortable. It's believing there is more to life, more possibilities, more potential. Having a greater impact. A no-limits life is waiting. Your time machine is you. You break the boundaries.

Brighter Days

The future driven educator is positive and hopeful. It's doing what's best for students in the long run. It's wanting good things FOR them and not just FROM them.

You foresee a future in every one of your students. They matter to you. You don't just see them for who they are right now. They will go so many places and do so many things. They will make an incredible impact on the world. And before these stories unfold, in their formative years, you can be an important influence on them. Your work matters.

So much hangs in the balance. If my dad hadn't persisted in getting through college, he never would've met my mom in seminary, and I wouldn't be writing this book. In 2008, my dad passed from this life. At his funeral, *I met his high school ag teacher.* I was blown away. My dad was 72 years old when he died. He was born in 1935. I didn't know any of his teachers were even still living.

My dad loved agriculture. That's what he thought he was going to do with his life. But I can only imagine that encouragement from mentors, like the ag teacher who came to his funeral, helped him to believe he could go to college. And his story eventually became my story and life marches on.

Stronger Learners

An important theme of this book and especially this chapter is to challenge you to push your limits as an educator and for you to challenge others to push their limits too. To create schools to meet the needs of our students, we must develop schools that meet the demands of the future. Are we organizing school based on what works best for kids or what works best for adults? Are we creating learning that was suited for another time or learning that will serve our students well into the future?

The answers to those questions cannot be overly simplistic. There are aspects of education that remain relevant even in changing times. The fundamentals of teaching and learning are much the same today as in the past and will continue to be vital in the future.

We must always honor excellence in teachers who have gone before. We must recognize that many of the same characteristics that made these teachers extraordinary in the past will also make a teacher excellent today. But the methods we use today must reflect what's happening in the world now and where the world is headed in the future. We must choose methods to help our students thrive tomorrow.

Here are a few closing thoughts on what authentic learning looks like for modern schools:

1. Learning should be transferable. The skills students learn should be ones that can be applied to a different context and still be useful. Students must be prepared to deal with circumstances that are completely new and rapidly changing. Therefore, the ability to adapt and learn is essential.

2. Learning needs to be as relevant as possible to the lives of our students. It needs to be personally meaningful. Learning should not just be about preparing for something later, but it should also be about making contributions now. Students should feel like the things they are doing in school are relevant to their lives now. They should have access to the curriculum in ways that are personally meaningful to them.

3. Educators should be concerned about getting kids excited about learning. The goal is for students to be more excited about learning tomorrow than they are today. In that, students need to develop their own questions, they need opportunities to be creative, and they need to express their curiosity. Some people think learning should be hard. I think it should be incredibly engaging and hard--challenging and fun.

If kids learn every standard but don't discover joy and passion in learning, we have failed them miserably. In Steven Johnson's (@stevenbjohnson) Ted Talk, he describes how play shaped the modern world. Many of the inventions we enjoyed were playful creations. He astutely concludes, "You'll discover the future where people are having the most fun."[3]

4. Content is only helpful when it is coupled with application. It accomplishes very little to develop students only as better test takers. Students need to be able to apply content to solve interesting problems, develop new ideas, and create new learning.

5. The system should seek to empower students and teachers as learners. This type of learning will result in more freedom than students and teachers have

experienced in the past. It will result in more choices about the how and what of learning, and it will result in more voice in the why and when of learning. When teachers and students are empowered as learners, engagement will increase. There will be increased agency and a desire to pursue excellence.

6. Students and teachers must still be held to high expectations of excellence. Teachers must not only develop strong relationships with students, but they must use the influence and opportunity they have to bring about more learning in students. Teachers must set the tone and model the way. Students must become partners in the process and gradually learn to take responsibility for their own growth and development. We want to create lifelong learners.

7. Learning should be more about creating incredible learning experiences for students. They should be doing tasks that reflect the type of work professionals do in the real world. Assessment should not just be quizzes and tests but should involve projects that are like what is done in professional settings. As students engage in these projects, they will learn a host of skills beyond the academic aspect of their learning. They will be stronger people, not just stronger students.

For Your Students

I'm guessing many students feel like school is a place where someone is always wanting something FROM them.

Turn in your homework.

Stop talking.

Get busy.

Walk in a straight line.

Follow instructions.

Pay attention.

Don't forget.

All the demands can really weigh heavily after a while. For some, I'm guessing school starts to feel like a huge burden. They don't see the relevance.

They feel like teachers are constantly wanting more FROM them, and they may not feel adequate to meet the expectations.

But maybe students don't understand the why behind all the expectations and requests. Maybe they don't realize that the best teachers, most teachers, in fact, don't really want something FROM students. They want good things FOR their students.

The expectations and demands are intended to help students succeed now and in the future. The demands aren't because teachers want to make things easier for themselves or want to make things harder for their students. Teachers are successful when students are successful.

So I think we should spend more time and effort showing students what it is we want FOR them. And maybe we should spend a little less time talking about what we want FROM them.

Of course, expectations are part of life. And if students are going to be successful, there will be accountability. But they should always be reminded that the accountability we provide is because we care. It's because we want good things FOR them.

Teachers who get the best FROM their students are the same teachers who show their students how much they care FOR them.

Try reminding your students you want these things FOR them...

FOR them to be leaders.

FOR them to develop strong character.

FOR them to believe in themselves.

FOR them to never stop growing.

FOR them to be more excited about learning when they leave us than when they started.

FOR them to demonstrate empathy and concern for others.

FOR them to learn from their mistakes.

FOR them to make the world a better place.

FOR them to learn more about who they are.

FOR them to build on their unique strengths.

FOR them to have hope.

FOR them to develop a great attitude.

FOR them to be adaptable to change.

FOR them to reach their potential.

FOR them to realize their dreams.

FOR them to feel like they belong.

FOR them to have healthy relationships.

FOR them to never give up.

FOR them to be curious, creative, and compassionate.

How Will You Be Remembered?

People are going to remember what you did. They will remember your contributions. Will they remember you as a nice person who was a good worker? Or will they remember you as someone who made an impact? Someone who pushed out into the future to show kids the way? Will you be a time capsule? Or will you be a time machine? There is absolutely nothing shameful about being a hard worker, who follows instructions and does the routine work efficiently. That work is important. But you have so much more to offer. There is brilliance inside you that can make the world a better place. But you must be willing to step forward and do more than the routine. You have to make your mark. You must invest all of you into what you do. It's time to make the most of your impact.

In *7 Habits of Successful People*, Stephen Covey challenges his readers with an exercise that is profound. You might find it unsettling or even slightly grim. But I urge you to read it carefully and thoughtfully. As you read the excerpt, consider how reflecting on this passage might be life changing for you too.[4]

> In your mind's eye, see yourself going to the funeral of a loved one. Picture yourself driving to the funeral parlor or chapel, parking the car, and getting out. As you walk inside the building, you notice the flowers, the soft organ music. You see the faces of friends and family you pass along the way. You feel the shared sorrow of losing, the joy of having known, that radiates from the hearts of the people there.

> As you walk down to the front of the room and look inside the casket, you suddenly come face to face with yourself. This is your funeral, three years from today. All these people have come to honor you, to express feelings of love and appreciation for your life.

As you take a seat and wait for the services to begin, you look at the program in your hand. There are to be four speakers. The first is from your family, immediate and also extended —children, brothers, sisters, nephews, nieces, aunts, uncles, cousins, and grandparents who have come from all over the country to attend. The second speaker is one of your friends, someone who can give a sense of what you were as a person. The third speaker is from your work or profession. And the fourth is from your church or some community organization where you've been involved in service.

Now think deeply. What would you like each of these speakers to say about you and your life? What kind of husband, wife, father, or mother would like their words to reflect? What kind of son or daughter or cousin? What kind of friend? What kind of working associate?

What character would you like them to have seen in you? What contributions, what achievements would you want them to remember? Look carefully at the people around you. What difference would you like to have made in their lives?

The 3-year timeline until your death is an important detail in the exercise. It creates a stronger sense of urgency. As educators, we should always have a sense of urgency too. We may be our students' best hope. But we only have so much time. We may not have the same opportunity to influence them next year. They will likely move on to a new classroom with a different teacher.

Although the funeral exercise is a great reflection for living a meaningful life, how might it be slightly modified to narrow the reflection for you as a teacher/educator? In a similar instance, what might your students say about you as their teacher? What would their parents say? How about the community you where you work? What is your legacy in that?

As I reflect on those questions, I am reminded of what's most important to me. And I am also reminded of things that might distract me from the most important things. The most valuable thing is how I treat people, all of them. People come first. I want to be the kind of person who is always learning, who lifts others up, and who treats people with kindness, care, and consideration.

It's easy to get distracted from the most important things. I am a person who also wants progress, who has goals, who is driven. If fact, in the past, there were times I was too focused on achieving and not tuned into the people around me. I am working hard to make sure that doesn't happen anymore.

I am convinced that reaching goals, making progress, and achieving success will be more likely to happen—mostly inevitable—if the first priority is people. If we treat people with all the care and concern we possibly can, we will see progress and success like never before.

I respect every person who works hard and gets stuff done. There is value in working hard and earning a living to support yourself and your loved ones. But teaching provides the opportunity to do far more than just earning a paycheck. It's more than a job. When teaching is your life's work, you can make a lasting difference. You can make an important contribution. Your legacy counts!

So think about it...

What really matters?

What keeps you up at night?

What makes you want to be a better teacher, principal, parent or friend?

I hope these questions are helpful as you think about your legacy and what's most important to you. Reflecting on what you really value is one of the best things you can do to find purpose and meaning in your life and work.

Look to the Future

Our work is not a destination. We must continue to grow and adapt quickly. The world is changing rapidly and will continue to change. In the past, there were spurts of rapid change. Now we are in an age of persistent change and rapid acceleration. The rate of change is so fast, it's very difficult to write an improvement plan that remains relevant. By the time you study and write a plan, it's too late.

We must get comfortable being uncomfortable and move fast. We don't have to abandon everything we know. There are things we need to keep doing. But there are things we need to stop doing. And there are definitely some things we must start doing too. We can't prepare students for the future if we are stuck in the past.

When I was growing up in West Kentucky, I had plenty of opportunities to work on the farm. Mostly I helped the neighbors in summer to earn spending money. I didn't get too many opportunities to drive the tractor. Usually, I had a hoe in my hands or was pulling suckers off tobacco plants. I wasn't hired to sit and ride a tractor very often.

But I did get a few chances to drive the tractor. If you want to plow a straight line you want to pick out something at the end of the row to focus your eyes on. You need to keep your eye on a tree or a fence post and keep your focus locked on the object out in the distance. Look far out in front. You want to pick out a spot and keep your eyes fixed there. And don't look back.

If you look back or don't keep your focus on a fixed object, your rows will not be straight. Your rows will be crooked and out of sorts. And it's like that for us as educators too. We need to keep our eyes way out in front. We need to stay true to what's most important. We cannot become distracted or look behind us, or we won't move forward with purpose.

All educators must be futurists because we are preparing students for more than today, we are preparing them for their future. We need to have an eye on tomorrow and help our students become adaptable learners. We must help them catch a vision for what's possible in their future. We must have that vision across the field and keep focused on what lies ahead.

We are living in a time that is fundamentally different than the one we grew up in. Our students are counting on us to prepare them for the future. We know there are problems that stand in the way. Our world is increasingly complex and uncertain. We can sit idle and think about what other people need to do, or we can step forward and work to create better schools.

I don't want to jump through hoops. I don't want to go through the motions. I don't want to just put in my time, do my job, and look forward to retirement. I never want to waste my time. I want to make an impact. I want to do my part to create a brighter future. We can do that every day. You are building futures every day.

Some professions build houses, or high-rise buildings, or magnificent bridges. But only teachers build bridges to a better future.

Some professions design the software, the hardware, or the workflow. But only teachers design learning experiences that kids will never forget.

Some professions make cars, or carpet, or cola. But only teachers make kids wonder, make them question, and make them want to learn more.[5]

Some professions grow our food. But only teachers help kids grow their minds.

Some professions create business, commerce, or trade that grow the economy. But only teachers develop leaders who will carry on our democracy.

Some professions are saving people's lives, but only teachers are changing lives.

Every profession is important. We need them all. And teachers play a role in helping students become whatever they will do in their futures. We know some of the jobs they will do don't even yet exist. So we must be adaptable. Are we creating schools that reflect the world we live in or the one we grew up in?

What will you do? What are three things you will change about your work as an educator after reading this book? What will you do in the next 10 days? In the next month? In the next year?

You can find more ideas for becoming a future driven educator by visiting the link below. I've included a detailed study guide for group discussion and action planning. I've also included a list of the books and articles that have had the greatest influence on my thinking. It provides additional resources for continuing your learning. By providing your email, I will send you updates from my blog. It provides a way for us to stay connected. I look forward to building stronger schools and a brighter future with all future driven educators.

GO TO HTTP://BIT.LY/FUTUREDRIVEN
TO DOWNLOAD THE BONUS CONTENT

Notes

Chapter 1

[1] "Future Ready Framework."
https://dashboard.futurereadyschools.org/framework.

Chapter 2

[1] Intelligence, Developments In artificial. "Technology could kill 5 million jobs by 2020." CNNMoney. http://money.cnn.com/2016/01/18/news/economy/job-losses-technology-five-million/.

[2] Pink, Daniel H. A whole new mind: how to thrive in the new conceptual age. London: Cyan, 2006.

[3] "The Inspirational Video Everyone Should Live By ▶ AmazingLife247." YouTube. September 13, 2013.
https://youtu.be/2x_Fl3NQVd4?list=FL6Cr8QtZdYSTWCwrmYe2MDg.

Chapter 3

[1] Deimler, Martin ReevesMike. "Adaptability: The New Competitive Advantage." Harvard Business Review. May 27, 2016.
https://hbr.org/2011/07/adaptability-the-new-competitive-advantage.

[2] "The Benefits of Being Adaptable." Business.com. http://www.business.com/entrepreneurship/how-well-do-you-handle-change-the-benefits-of-being-adaptable/.

[3] "Netflix Refines Its DVD Business, Even as Streaming Unit Booms." The New York Times. July 26, 2015. http://www.nytimes.com/2015/07/27/business/while-its-streaming-service-booms-netflix-streamlines-old-business.html.

[4] Rosenbaum, Steven. "The Happiness Culture: Zappos Isn't a Company - It's a Mission." Fast Company. July 30, 2012. https://www.fastcompany.com/1657030/happiness-culture-zappos-isnt-company-its-mission.

[5] Bellis, Rich. "Here's Why The Freelancer Economy Is On The Rise." Fast Company. August 13, 2015. https://www.fastcompany.com/3049532/the-future-of-work/heres-why-the-freelancer-economy-is-on-the-rise.

[6] Friedman, Thomas L. "Opinion | How to Get a Job at Google." The New York Times. February 22, 2014. https://www.nytimes.com/2014/02/23/opinion/sunday/friedman-how-to-get-a-job-at-google.html.

[7] "Beyond Ditching the Desks, 9 Creative Ways to Avoid The Cemetery Effect for All Classrooms." Tom Murray. http://thomascmurray.com/cemeteryeffect/.

[8] "Student Voice and Choice Through Innovation and, Yes, Cardboard." John Linney. http://schoolclimateinstitute.com/071-student-voice/#more-1469

Chapter 4

[1] Nesloney, Todd, and Adam Welcome. *Kids deserve it!: pushing boundaries and challenging conventional thinking*. San Diego, CA: Dave Burgess Consulting, Inc., 2016.

[2] Not his real name gang.

[3] Hattie, John. Visible learning: a synthesis of over 800 meta-analyses relating to achievement. London: Routledge, 2010.

[4] Allday, R. Allan, and Kerri Pakurar. "Effects of Teacher Greetings on Student On-task Behavior." *Journal of Applied Behavior Analysis* 40, no. 2 (Summer 2007): 317-20. https://www.ncbi.nlm.nih.gov/pmc/articles/PMC1885415/.

[5] Roehlkepartain, Eugene, Kent Pekel, Amy Syvertsen, Jenna Sethi, Theresa Sullivan, and Peter Scales. "Relationships First: Creating Connections that Help Young People Thrive." 2017. http://v.fastcdn.co/u/73824624/13516863-0-FINALRelationships-F.pdf.

[6] Barth, Ronald. "Improving Relationships Within the Schoolhouse." Educational Leadership. http://www.ascd.org/publications/educational-leadership/mar06/vol63/num06/Improving-Relationships-Within-the-Schoolhouse.aspx.

[7] Provenzano, Nicholas. "3 Ways to Make Meaningful Connections With Your Students." Edutopia. February 24, 2014. https://www.edutopia.org/blog/make-meaningful-connections-with-students-nick-provenzano.

[8] "Want Better Faculty Meetings? Start Here." THE TEMPERED RADICAL. February 04, 2017. http://blog.williamferriter.com/2017/02/04/want-better-faculty-meetings-start-here/.

[9] Coyle, Daniel. The talent code: Greatness isnt born. It's grown. London: Arrow, 2010.

Chapter 5

[1] Burgess, Dave. Teach like a pirate: increase student engagement, boost your creativity, and transform your life as an educator. San Diego, CA: Dave Burgess Consulting, Inc., 2012.

[2] Sztabnik, Brian. "The 8 Minutes That Matter Most." Edutopia. January 05, 2015. https://www.edutopia.org/blog/8-minutes-that-matter-most-brian-sztabnik.

Chapter 7

[1] "Whoever is doing the talking is doing the learning." Blanchard LeaderChat. January 24, 2011. https://leaderchat.org/2011/01/24/whoever-is-doing-the-talking-is-doing-the-learning/.

[2] "Danielson Group » The Framework." Danielson Group The Framework Comments. http://www.danielsongroup.org/framework/.

Chapter 8

[1] Goleman, Daniel, and Daniel Goleman, Richard E. Boyatzis, and Annie McKee. "What Makes a Leader?" Harvard Business Review. July 18, 2017. https://hbr.org/2004/01/what-makes-a-leader.

[2] FRIEDMAN, THOMAS L. THANK YOU FOR BEING LATE: an optimists guide to thriving in the age of accelerations. S.l.: PENGUIN BOOKS, 2017.

Chapter 10

[1] Fox, Stuart. "Moscow's Stray Dogs Evolving Greater Intelligence, Including a Mastery of the Subway." Popular Science. January 21, 2010. http://www.popsci.com/science/article/2010-01/moscows-stray-dogs-evolving-greater-intelligence-wolf-characteristics-and-mastery-subway.

[2] Wiliam, Dylan. *Embedded formative assessment*. Bloomington, IN: Solution Tree Press, 2018.

[3] "Knowledge Doubling Every 12 Months, Soon to be Every 12 Hours." Industry Tap. June 13, 2017. http://www.industrytap.com/knowledge-doubling-every-12-months-soon-to-be-every-12-hours/3950.

Chapter 11

[1] Hobson, Katherine. "Feeling Lonely? Too Much Time On Social Media May Be Why." NPR. March 06, 2017. http://www.npr.org/sections/health-shots/2017/03/06/518362255/feeling-lonely-too-much-time-on-social-media-may-be-why.

[2] "Care to Learn » About." Care to Learn. http://caretolearnfund.org/about/.

Chapter 12

[1] Project Red Research Overview. http://one-to-oneinstitute.org/research-overview.

Chapter 13

[1] Couros, George. The innovators mindset empower learning, unleash talent, and lead a culture of creativity. San Diego, CA: Dave Burgess Consulting, 2015.

Chapter 14

[1] Pink, Daniel H. *Drive: the surprising truth about what motivates us*. New York: Riverhead Books, 2012.

[2] "Bruce Farrer, thank you for inspiring us | WestJet Above and Beyond Stories." YouTube. November 03, 2014.
https://youtu.be/oeX1H7ajOvQ?list=FL6Cr8QtZdYSTWCwrmYe2MDg.

[3] November, Alan C. Who owns the learning?: preparing students for success in the digital age. Bloomington, IN: Solution Tree Press, 2012.

Chapter 15

[1] Kriegel, Robert J., and Louis Patler. If it aint broke-- break it!: and other unconventional wisdom for a changing business world. Melbourne: Business Library, 1994.

[2] North Point. http://northpoint.org/messages/heroes-2017/just-be-you/.

[3] Johnson, Steven. "The playful wonderland behind great inventions." Steven Johnson: The playful wonderland behind great inventions | TED Talk. https://www.ted.com/talks/steven_johnson_how_play_leads_to_great_inventions.

[4] Covey, Stephen R. The 7 habits of highly effective people. Provo, UT: Franklin Covey, 1998.

[5] Mali, Taylor. "What teachers make." Taylor Mali: What teachers make | TED Talk. https://www.ted.com/talks/taylor_mali_what_teachers_make.

ABOUT THE AUTHOR

David Geurin is the proud principal and lead learner of Bolivar High School, a National Blue Ribbon School and *Home of the Liberators*. He is committed  to developing future-driven, student-centered schools. He shares his ideas on learner empowerment, leadership, and innovation via social media, blogging, speaking, and consulting.

In 2008, he earned a doctorate in Educational Leadership and Policy Analysis from the University of Missouri.

More recently, he was recognized by the National Association of Secondary School Principals (NASSP) as a 2017 National Digital Principal of the Year. See more from David at www.davidgeurin.com or follow him on Twitter (@DavidGeurin).

CPSIA information can be obtained
at www.ICGtesting.com
Printed in the USA
LVHW021240080521
686870LV00003B/112